Wade Hampton

A VOICE FROM SOUTH CAROLINA

A Narrative of the Upstate During
Reconstruction and Redemption

with a
Journal of a Reputed Ku-Klux

and an
Appendix

by
John A. Leland, Ph.D.

THE CONFEDERATE
REPRINT COMPANY
☆　☆　☆　☆
WWW.CONFEDERATEREPRINT.COM

A Voice From South Carolina
A Narrative of the Upstate During
Reconstruction and Redemption
by John Adams Leland, Ph.D.

Originally Published in 1879 by
Walker, Evans, and Cogswell
Charleston, South Carolina

Reprint Edition © 2016
The Confederate Reprint Company
Post Office Box 2027
Toccoa, Georgia 30577
www.confederatereprint.com

Cover and Interior Design by
Magnolia Graphic Design
www.magnoliagrapicdesign.com

ISBN-13: 978-1945848070
ISBN-10: 1945848073

Dedicated to the Women of South Carolina

PREFACE

☆   ☆   ☆   ☆

The following pages have grown into the proportions of a book, without much design on the part of the author. His purpose, at first, was merely to transcribe the journal of his "jail experience," at the request of some particular friends. This, he found, would be unsatisfactory, without some account of the condition of things in Laurens County, at the time of his arrest.

But the state of things in Laurens was anomalous, resulting from causes which affected the whole State alike. A resumé of Reconstruction in South Carolina, therefore, seemed necessary; and thus, step by step, he was led back to the deluge of Secession.

The narrative was begun in 1874, and continued, from time to time, till the beginning of 1876. The writer then closed with the twelfth chapter; and made efforts to publish in that centennial year. As all these efforts failed, the MS. was still on hand, when the wonderful campaign of "Hampton and Home Rule" brought about another Revolution. This rendered two additional chapters necessary, to come down to the date of the regeneration of the State.

The author now sends forth these *disjecta membra* with many misgivings. No one can see the defects of the work more plainly than he does himself; but the remedy would be to re-write the whole, and such a reconstruction might prove as complete a failure and wreck as the one he has attempted to describe.

7

Begging indulgence for this, his first attempt at authorship, he earnestly requests a patient perusal of all the facts herein recorded, with the assurance that there is

Nothing extenuate.
Nor aught set down in malice.

CONTENTS

PART ONE:
Before Hampton

CHAPTER ONE
Introductory

CHAPTER TWO
After the War

CHAPTER THREE
Reconstruction

CHAPTER FOUR
Reconstruction in Laurens County

CHAPTER ELEVEN
Recent Reconstruction

CHAPTER TWELVE
Centennial Sentiments

PART TWO:
After Hampton

POSTSCRIPT ONE
Hampton's Campaign

POSTSCRIPT TWO
Redemption and Home Rule

APPENDIX

PART ONE:
Before Hampton

CHAPTER ONE

☆　☆　☆　☆

Introductory

South Carolina can proudly point to a galaxy of historic names, who have illustrated her fame in every period of her past history. Through these her voice has already been heard in tones which will reach the latest posterity.

In the dark days of the Revolution, this voice could be heard in such clarion notes as her Moultries, her Sumters, and her Marions could utter, to electrify to new life her people, though overrun and all but conquered.

In the formation of the government, it has been heard, in no faltering accents, from her Pinckneys, her Laurenses, her Rutledges and her Heywards – equals among equals – statesmen, who were jealous of her liberty so dearly purchased. These only consented to her association with her sister colonies, when they thought this liberty was hedged in by every safeguard which human wisdom could devise.

It has been heard in the halls of State and Federal legislation, from the tongues of Calhoun, Hayne, McDuffie, Preston, and a long list of worthies, whose names will ever adorn the annals of the past. Giants in intellect, who could embellish profound and ennobling statesmanship and patriotism, with unsullied integrity, and the purity of the high-toned gentleman.

But this potent voice has long been hushed, and her approaching "centennial year" will find her in habiliments of mourn-ing – silent and sad. Most of her sisters who began the race with her, and very many of those younger ones, who are but of yester-day, and who owe so much to her sacrifice of blood and treasure, will then be rejoicing in their prosperity, and have already invited the whole world to witness their progress and their greatness. She, almost alone of the "Old Thirteen," will turn her face to the wall, and will feel no responsive throb to the rejoicings over this national jubilee.

In one short century, she seems to have run her whole career of rise, progress, decline and fall. She has the same bright sky above her, as in her palmiest days; the same broad rivers flowing from her mountains to the seaboard; the same fertile soil and genial climate; but

'Tis Greece; but living Greece no more,

yet, unlike ancient Greece, how short-lived has been her glory!

Her most bitter enemies must admit that her, so-called, leaders have maintained a dignified silence since her fall. Even those who watch so assiduously to catch up and pervert every chance expression of Ex-President Davis, have found nothing to report from them. These gentlemen show that it is the part of true manhood to *endure* what is unavoidable, as well as to *dare;* and that fortitude is, in many respects, a higher virtue than bravery.

This "Voice from South Carolina," comes from one of her humble sons, whose earnest desire is to cling but the closer to her side in the day of her humiliation. He feels irresistibly impelled to publish to the world that the grand old State, de-clared to be free, sovereign and independent, an hundred years ago, is now deposed, gagged, and trampled in the dust. Her seat and name has been usurped by a brazen-faced strumpet, foisted upon her "high places" by the hands of strangers; her proud mon-uments of the past, all begrimed and vandalized; her sacred trea-sury thrown wide open to the insatiable rapacity of thieves and robbers; and her bright escutcheon blackened by every crime known to the decalogue.

All these, too, have been the legitimate fruits of deliberate legislation on the part of her sister States, in Congress assembled; peopled, like herself, by the descendants of that glorious old Anglo-Saxon race, whose achievements on this continent have filled the world with amazement and admiration. Could our common ancestors ever have foreseen this? Can posterity ever account for the "madness of the hour," in States having the same lineage, combining to drive one of their number from the folds of civilization into the dark despotism of African rule? And yet, South Carolina to-day presents the terrible picture of a great American State abandoned to the tender mercies of her former slaves, exasperated and maddened by the teachings and guidance of foreign mercenaries and native desperadoes.

Her living sons, whom she once delighted to honor, and whose hearts still throb with undying love and devotion, are powerless and voiceless. For them there is no arena amid scenes like these, and no tribunal to which they can appeal. The indications now are, that the grand old type of the "Southern gentleman" will soon pass from the stage of active life to the dark mausoleum of the great Past. Hereafter he is to be associated with the "Patriarchs," the "Areopagites," and the "Conscript-Fathers," who have, from age to age, illustrated the higher and nobler qualities of our common humanity. With him, State-pride was his idolatry, and honor was his life. Born to command, he was ever too high above the venal place-man and office-seeker, ever to stoop to the low arts of the mere politician and demagogue. What Webster said of Calhoun, in his noble eulogy over that great statesman, might be said of the whole class, of whom Mr. Calhoun was the honored exponent: "Nothing low or selfish ever came near the head or heart of Calhoun."

Those who carped at this type of character, mainly from natural want of appreciation, disguised their envy or their fear under the cant phrases of "Southern chivalry," "Slaveocracy," &c. But to this class is mainly due all the statesmanship and dignity which have adorned our government. Since these have been excluded from the councils of the nation, congressional legislation has become little more than the registering of party edicts. Railroad rings, Credit Mobilier rings, back-pay grabs, &c., had already nauseated the public, when the recent investigations bid fair to bring bribery, fraud and corruption to the very threshold of the Chief Executive of the Republic. In the days of the sway of "Southern chivalry," such mortifying and disgusting exhibitions in our high places would have been moral impossibilities.

And what have these reconstructionists given us in the place of a civilization so ruthlessly destroyed? What type of citizen, in the once proud old commonwealth of South Carolina, can now look for place or preferment? The phrase used to be, to "aspire" to posts of profit and trust, but in this complete revolution, the aspirant must learn to stoop to the very lowest arts of the demagogue. He must so debase himself in political pollution that he can never again look his former associates in the face, or claim the smallest remnant of self respect. "Dirt eating," in regular and constantly increasing rations, is the only diet to change his nature, and fit him to become a loyal citizen of this mongrel Dahomey.

And what hope is there for the rising generation, in a civilization like this? The land-marks of the fathers all obliterated, and the teachings of history, as well as of the fireside, all reversed. What can all these avail, when he sees vice rolling in wealth, and virtue covered with rags; the liar and thief clothed in the regalia of the highest offices, and the true and patriotic happy if only they can escape the dungeon; and he who can stoop the lowest in infamy, reaping the largest pecuniary rewards, while the pure and the noble are worn down by daily toil for their daily bread.

There is a terrible weight of responsibility somewhere for this horrible state of things in a Christian land and in the full light of the civilization of the nineteenth century. The true-born son of the soil feels that it is not on him. In the great national conflict, of which this was the direful sequel, he was only carrying out the teachings of his Revolutionary sires, and the prompt-ings of his own manhood. To avert these very calamities he has sacrificed all, save his honor, and voiceless and powerless, he can only endure.

The "bills of mortality" tell a sad tale of many of these who had passed the meridian of their powers; reminding us, mournfully, of what is so often sung thoughtlessly:

> For Freedom now so seldom wakes,
> The only throb she gives,
> Is when some heart indignant breaks,
> To tell that still she lives.

In all the grief and mourning of our stricken State over her "Lost Cause," there are found no tears of penitence. She still proudly points to the records of 1860; and it is her chief solace that she has attempted *all* in her power to avert these very calamities, which she then believed to be inevitable.

It is not the design of this little book to undertake a vindication of the right of secession. This has already been done by far abler pens, and the verdict of impartial history may calmly be awaited on that point. The writer, however, must be pardoned for giving his testimony against the charge that the act of secession in South Carolina was the work of political leaders. On the contrary, it was one of the grandest spectacles of the unanimous uprising of a whole people the world has ever seen. The "leaders" hesitated at the bold step; the people pushed them aside and came squarely up to the issue. The high and the low, the rich and the poor, the male and the female, the clergy and the laity, the brave and the timid, all, all were of one accord in the "Rebellion" of 1860. The tories in 1776 who still adhered to the British crown, were as one hundred to one, when compared to the "Union men" in 1860, in point of numbers; and in character and standing, were vastly superior.

When the passions of men shall have had time to cool down, and the deadly hate so long cherished shall have died out with the generation who have fomented it, the course of South Carolina, in what is called her secession mania, will not appear

so reckless and mad as our present (Northern) school histories represent it. The moral mania on the other side will then come more prominently forward, and even
at the madness that ruled the hour. Slavery was the occasion of all this mania on both sides, and posterity will know the *facts* of the case, without being distempered by morbid sentiment.

A calm review of these facts will show, that as long as slavery and the slave-trade continued to be sources of profit, the conscience of the majority slept quietly enough over their great enormities. After a more full development of their appropriate industries, it was found that the slave was an incubus, and he was quietly shipped and sold where his services were regarded as still indispensable. Being thus happily relieved of his presence, and reimbursed for his pecuniary value, they abolished the institution in their own States; and these same consciences *then* became most painfully sensitive to the sins of their neighbors, on whom they had palmed their whole load of fancied guilt. It will not *then* be forgotten, that, at the time of the adoption of the Constitution, *all* the States were slave-holding, with a single exception; that slavery was fully recognized and guaranteed in the fundamental law of the land, and that all efforts at its abolition were really acts of disloyalty to the government. Yet an antislavery sentiment did spring up, at first confined to those despicable and trouble-some spirits to be found in every country, who attempt to draw off public attention from their own misdeeds by a great outcry against the faults of others for which they are in no sense respon-sible. But this little cloud, at first no bigger than a man's hand, afterwards darkened and blackened the whole political sky. A generation arose who had imbibed with their mother's milk this moral prejudice, and had been incessantly taught from their earli-est infancy, in the home-circle, in the school, in the public prints, in every harangue before the people, and even in the Sanctuary of God, to regard slavery as the sum of all iniquities, and a blot upon the body politic, which it was their mission to remove.

Is it to be wondered at that a generation thus indoctrinated should early begin a crusade against this, the greatest of national sins? And when they themselves became the actors upon the public arena, what limit could be fixed to their moral mania? Every political question became subordinate to this, and no aspirant for popular favor could hope for success without adopting as his own the watchword *carthago est delenda.* This tornado of fanaticism overspread whole States, and soon controlled the public sentiment of the dominant section of the Union. Already was a President elected by a strictly sectional vote, and there was every probability that a majority in Congress would soon be secured, which, by its omnipotence in controlling every other department of government, would leave no ground for hope.

A mighty revolution was thus effected, and the government of the United States, based on a written Constitution, was to be changed into a huge party engine, to carry out hostile sectional policies. The Constitution had already become a dead letter, and the will of the majority was to become the supreme law of the land. Congress, so jealously checked by the fathers, through the co-ordinate branches of the executive and judiciary, was henceforth to exercise the omnipotence claimed by the Parliament of Great Britain.

This was not the union for which South Carolina had made such sacrifices, neither was this the government for the maintenance of which she had plighted her faith and her sacred honor. She had unanimously entered into a solemn league and covenant with homogeneous States and allies, in solemn convention assembled; again, in solemn convention assembled, she as unanimously withdrew from this union, when it was revolutionized into a consolidated government, controlled by a hostile party. And yet this solemn and formal expression of the sovereign will of the whole people of a State, has been branded as a "Rebellion"; and the secession of ten States from a revolutionized Union, has been stigmatized as an "Insurrection"!

Twice before, since the formation of the government, had the State gone into convention from her jealousy of oppression and zeal for States' Rights; but on each of these occasions her people were nearly equally divided. This was not owing to any difference of opinion as to the wrongs complained of, but on the question whether the remedy would be best found within or without the Union. In 1860, those who hoped for any redress within the Union were the merest handful, held back more from pride of opinion than from any real love to the government as it then was.

As to the convention itself, take the following sketch of it, drawn by a master pen. The Rev. Dr. Thornwell stood too high in public estimation ever to stoop to flattery; and was too great a devotee to truth ever to exaggerate in the smallest particular. In an article written for the *Southern Presbyterian Review,* of 1860, and headed, "The State of the Country," he said:

"That there was a cause, and an adequate cause, might be presumed from the character of the convention which passed the Ordinance of Secession, and the perfect unanimity with which it was done. The convention was not a collection of politicians and demagogues. It was not a conclave of defeated place-hunters, who sought to avenge their disappointment by the ruin of their country. It was a body of grave, sober and venerable men, selected from every pursuit in life, and distinguished, most of them, in their respective spheres, by every quality which can command confidence and respect. It embraced the wisdom, moderation and integrity of the bench; the learning and prudence of the bar; and the eloquence and learning of the pulpit. It contained retired planters, scholars and gentlemen, who stood aloof from the turmoil and ambition of public life, and were devoting an elegant leisure to the culture of their minds, and to quiet and unobtrusive schemes of Christian philanthropy. There were men in that convention utterly incapable of low and selfish schemes, who, in the calm serenity of their judgments, were as unmoved by the waves of popular passion and excitement, as the everlasting granite by the billows that roll against it. There were men there who would listen to no voice but the voice of reason; and would bow to no authority but what they believed to be the authority of God. There were men there who would not be controlled by 'uncertain opinion,' nor be betrayed into 'sudden counsels;' men who would act from nothing, in the noble language of Milton, 'but from mature wisdom, deliberate virtue, and the dear affection of the public good.' That convention, in the character of its members, deserves every syllable of the glowing panegyric which Milton pronounced upon the immortal Parliament of Great Britain which taught the nations of the earth that resistance to tyrants was obedience to God. Were it not invidious, we might single out names, which, wherever they are known, are regarded as synonymous with purity, probity, magnanimity and honor. It was a noble body, and all their proceedings were in harmony with their high character. In the midst of intense agitation and excitement, they were calm, cool, collected and self-possessed. They deliberated without passion, and concluded without rashness. They sat with closed doors, that the tumult of the population might not invade the sobriety of their minds. If a stranger could have passed from the stirring scenes with which the streets of Charleston were alive, into the calm and quiet sanctuary of this venerable council, he would have been impressed with the awe and veneration which subdued the rude Gaul, when he first beheld, in senatorial dignity, the Conscript-Fathers of Rome. That in such a body there was not a single vote against the Ordinance of Secession; that there was not only no dissent, but the assent was cordial and thoroughgoing, is a strong presumption that the measure was justified by the clearest and sternest necessities of justice and of right. That such an assembly should have inaugurated a radical revolution in all the external relations of the State, in the face of acknowledged dangers, and at the risk of enormous sacrifices, and should have done it gravely, soberly, dispassionately, deliberately, and yet have done it without cause, transcends all the measures of probability. Whatever else may be said of it, it certainly must be admitted that this solemn act of South Carolina was well considered."

CHAPTER TWO

☆ ☆ ☆ ☆

After the War

It is impossible to conceive of a more gloomy and cheerless welcome than that which awaited the Confederate soldier returning to his home in South Carolina. If it was in the broad track of Sherman across the State, two chimneys alone, in most cases, would mark the place of his once happy dwelling; or, if his house was spared, his famished family could only welcome him to a shelter, a forlorn picture of desolation. If his house was gone, the returned soldier would have to travel many a weary mile in search of his loved ones, who had been compelled to seek for food and shelter elsewhere. There was no hope of hospitality in the immediate vicinity, where every morsel was prized far more than gold had been in former years.

And when his house was spared, he would have to listen to harrowing accounts of officers and privates of the invading army indulging themselves in such acts of cruelty and barbarism as seemed to belong to another age, and another country. The "standing order," in the whole march across the State, was to pillage and burn to the ground every abandoned dwelling; but, if occupied, then to pillage, but not to burn.

Exuno disce omnes. The indignant wife would have to tell of the rude entering of rough and boisterous squads. Some would go to the out-buildings to learn from the servants the circumstances of the family – the first question always being as to the probability of any hid treasure. If they found cause to suspect that money had actually been secreted, how the soldier's heart would fire at the dastardly means resorted to to extort confession. Pistols ready cocked were held to the head of the defenceless wife, or the aged father would be taken to some convenient place, whatever its character, and hung by the neck, until life was nearly extinct. If these failed, then he would be whipped until either their purpose was gained, or the victim deprived of consciousness. In the meantime, other parties would be equally busy. The smokehouse would soon be broken open, and the family carriage, with horses attached, stood ready for the unusual freight. Hams, sides of bacon, corn, flour, all the supplies so carefully guarded, and economically used, would be piled in the carriage, till the load would reach the roof, then horses and carriage, with supplies, would disappear, the horses going at a furious rate.

While some would be busy killing the cattle and poultry of every kind, another party would swagger into the dwelling and ransack it from cellar to garret. After breaking into every place that had a lock, and throwing out of the windows whatever their friends below could put to any possible use, they would call the servants in, to help themselves to whatever might strike their fancies. Then returning to the room where they had left the whole family, of wife, daughters and children, cowering in one corner, they would utter the coarsest abuse of husband and brothers, and gloat over their terror and their tears. Not satisfied yet, with this, their manly revenge, they would lead in the servant girls, all dressed in the finest they could find in their young mistress's wardrobes, and dance with them over carpets, soon to be ripped into suitable breadths for saddle-cloths. The piano, which furnished the jingle for the dance, would afterwards be disjointed by their bayonets, and the fragments thrown out of the window. On leaving the house, if they found anything that could be of any possible use to the family, they would most wantonly destroy it – sometimes emptying barrels of sorghum into the watering troughs, and, ripping open feather-beds and pillows, discharge their contents into this, and with their bayonets stir the whole into a thorough mixture. If any domestic animal was left, it was shot down and rendered unfit for food.

It required many hours for this immense army to march by, but when the last squad of bummers departed there would be absolutely nothing left which could contribute to food or any other family comfort. The servants, of course, were all enticed to follow the army, and, for days, such families would subsist on selected parts of the animals so wantonly killed and cut to pieces, and on corn scattered on the ground where the cavalry horses had been last fed – there were no hogs left now, to dispute possession of such relics.

Such was the tale of desolation for the returned soldier, if his home had been anywhere in that wide belt so thoroughly ploughed by Sherman, from the Georgia line, near Savannah, to the North Carolina line.

If his home had been in Columbia, his heart would be wrung by the recital of those terrible and horrible scenes of that stormy February night, of which the world has already heard so much. A whole city burned to the ground, including the State house and other public buildings, and all in half a night, was no very wonderful feat for so large a body of incendiaries. This treat had been promised his army, by Sherman, all through his weary march through Georgia, and his men enjoyed it, as only such an army could be expected to do. None but those who witnessed their bacchanalian orgies can fully appreciate them, and form a just conception how nearly those clothed in human forms can personate devils incarnate.

If he had once lived in ease and luxury in those favored sea islands, or if his home had once been in the midst of the culture, wealth and refinement of Beaufort and its vicinity, a heart-sickening account of ruin and poverty awaited him. He would hear how the fall of Port Royal, early in the war, left them exposed to the inroads of enemies, just a little less barbarous than Sherman's bummers. These did not use the torch as their favorite weapon, but were very little behind them in the cowardly revenge of insulting the vanquished. They were told to stay at home but on condition of full equality with their former slaves. In this, too, all possible collision must be avoided, as they were bound to favor the "wards of the nation." Of course, in this early stage of the war, with the whole State before them, and yet confident of final success, these natives would submit to no such humiliating conditions, and nearly all that section of country was abandoned to negroes and camp-followers. Their exodus was a sad one, and the consequences were deplorable and lasting. Those who could afford it, chartered steamers and removed their families and furniture to Charleston for refuge. Others, and much the greater part, left their all behind them, and escaped with their families alone. Those who had removed to Charleston fared no better. The great fire which followed soon after, and swept diagonally across the city, from the Cooper to the Ashley, and over the quarter where they had just domiciled, consumed in one night the accumulations of long years of labor and economy. The sufferings of these people were more deplorable than those of any other section of the State. Their estates thus abandoned were seized by their negro slaves and by strangers, and in most cases have passed entirely from their possession. What from dividing them out by military order, and from selling for United States taxes, the titles even have passed into other hands, and they are left destitute. Impoverished and ruined in fortune, they even now can be found scattered over the State, in circumstances of great destitution.

And what was their crime? Simply their living in the neighborhood of the first post that fell into the hands of the enemy in open war. Was this civilized warfare, to seize and appropriate to government officials whole areas of the territory, and all the private property, merely because the military post near them had fallen? We will have to look far back into the annals of the past to find any precedent for this course, and only succeed when on the confines of the dark ages.

When the returned soldier had once seen his premises, fenceless, and grown up in weeds, the doors and blinds of his house all gone, used up for fire-wood, the portraits of his ancestors taking the places of fire-screens, and even their tombstones, in Beaufort, applied to other and meaner purposes, his heart would sink too low to rise again to any hope of restoring the past. But when he would find the whole vicinity given up to a motley gang, and miscegenation and open concubinage the prevailing habits of the new settlers, his impulse was to put his family and all he held dear as far as possible from this moral pestilence. It could be his home no longer!

And poor old Charleston, the once proud metropolis of the State, the seat of elegance and refinement, and of a hospitality so world-wide in its fame! Like all her sons, the returned soldier had cherished a filial affection for his native city, unknown to a migratory people. When he had gone forth as a hopeful volunteer, and all through the hardships, fightings and privations of a long war, the most cheering picture before him was old Charleston – restored to her commercial importance. Though he knew that the course of events before the war had caused her to subside into a mere dependency on her Northern rivals, still he knew that it had not always been so. There had been a time when she held proud rank with these same rivals, and her commerce, too, had whitened foreign seas. He knew that about the time of the Revolution she had had six large ship-yards in active operation; and as early as between 1740 and 1779, she had built twenty-five square-rigged vessels, besides very many coasters for the West India trade and that of the Atlantic coast. Under new and brighter auspices, why might not prosperity not only be restored to her, but be greatly enhanced? The Southern Confederacy once established, why might not this ancient city become the New York of the New Republic?

These had been his day-dreams for four long years, but what was his awaking? Her wharves either torn up, or rotted down from disuse, her princely mansions, which had been venerated for generations, all ragged from bursting shells, and shattered in the unprecedented bombardment of those long and weary years, her streets covered with coatings of grass, and her public squares so grown up in weeds that the wild beasts from the country found ample shelter there through the demolished enclosures.

But grand even in ruins, proudly had she defied all the enemy's engines of destruction for more than two long years, and only fell when her citizen soldiers marched out to defend more vital points. It was some days before the evacuation was even known to the enemy, and then he marched in, only to triumph over women and children, in their battered dwellings and blackened walls. But here, too, they assumed all their peculiar "rights of the conquerors," and we have the same sickening tales of private property seized for government use, or no known use at all, and of private rights insulted and outraged by the elevation of the slave to the position of master.

Just here, the writer would pause to notice some most ungenerous flings against the energy and enterprise of this stricken city, graced by those modern cant phrases of "Bourbonism," "old fogyism," "fossilized," &c., and all this accompanied by glowing contrasts, pictured in the cases of Chicago and Boston. That while these two great cities had built up their waste places, as if by magic, the traces of the fire which occurred in Charleston more than thirteen years ago are still manifest in the vacant lots and crumbling walls which mark its progress.

These carpers should remember that the business of Charleston was not only paralyzed by the war, but was "dead, twice dead, plucked up by the roots"! Savannah and some of her other Southern neighbors were revived by the return of some of their strongest firms, with increased capitals, who had removed to places of safety at the beginning of hostilities; but there was no such recuperation for this old city. Her merchants and business men stood in their own lot through the whole strife, and were all prostrated together. They, therefore, had to begin, as the phrase is, *from the stump.* Even in these circumstances, the enterprise and grit of her citizens would soon have restored a measure of prosperity, if they could have had a fair field for their development. But, just then, she was turned over to African rule, both State and municipal; and what people could have flourished under such insatiate and incessant draining? Sampson, shorn of his locks, was not more completely in the hands of *his* Philistines.

But to come back to our returned soldier. Even in the most favored sections of the State, scenes of desolation and decay awaited him. Four long years of rigid blockade from without, and of extortion and rapacity from heartless "speculators" from within, had blackened all the picture his imagination had painted of home, and, worst of all, his rights of citizenship were all gone. The old State was peopled by negroes and "paroled prisoners of war," without even the forms of civilized government. Her courthouses were all closed, her Governor was himself a prisoner in the Dry Tortugas, and even municipal government of incorporated towns was all suspended. It afforded a striking evidence of the law-abiding character of her citizens, that, in this complete interregnum of all constituted authority, which continued for so many months, there should be so few infractions of the public peace; and that all things should go on as orderly and peacefully as they did.

The negroes had not yet been tampered with, and were as obedient and faithful as they had been during the war. The whole history of the State, during this short period, was a practical illustration of the power of public opinion in maintaining order, and in preserving the peace of the community. Sometimes a small garrison of colored troops would be marched to some point in the interior, and then a series of petty annoyances would begin and expand. The little "Lieutenant commanding" would be judge, jury and sheriff, in his little "Military Court," and *fines* were almost exclusively his penalties. How near these fines ever got to the United States treasury has never been ascertained, and probably never will be. All the cases, it may be safely said, were of colored plaintiffs against white defendants, on charges of "assault and battery." The negroes would be put up to all manner of insolence by their brethren in uniform and their friends, and when a blow, or other punishment, would thus be provoked, the culprit would soon be seized by an armed squad, and taken to headquarters (Lieutenant commanding), whether by day or by night, and irrespective of distance or state of health. This petty tyranny was excessively annoying, particularly as these fines, varying from twenty to one hundred dollars, had to be promptly met, when there was no money in the country. Heirlooms and old family plate had in most instances to be sacrificed, and the "Court," too often, became the purchaser.

And following hard upon these intolerable annoyances, came the "Freedman's Bureau," emerging from its embryo state on the Sea Islands, and spreading its filthy meshes all over the State. These were, at first, mere swindling machines in the hands of sharpers. Afterwards party contrivances were superadded for the political bondage of the black man, far more galling than those world-abused "chains of slavery." These man-traps furnished appropriate schooling for that rapacious crew who afterwards revelled in the treasury of the State. Here Scott and his congenial colleagues received that impervious coating over everything like conscience, which fitted him and them for the open robbing of public funds.

By way of gossiping postscript to this chapter, it may be remarked that these colored garrisons, so profusely scattered over the State, rejoiced in the high-sounding titles of "57th," "59th," &c., "*Massachusetts* Regiments," and some explanation seems necessary for the fact that Massachusetts Regiments were so exclusively selected to march over South Carolina soil, *after the surrender.*

In the malarial regions near Port Royal, including most of the Sea Islands, the slaves employed in the culture of rice and cotton constituted the very lowest type of the African race in the State. They were for the most part the immediate descendants of the latest importations of native Africans brought to our shores, in New England vessels, up to 1808 – the limit fixed in the Constitution to the "slave trade." These were generally worked in large gangs, having but little intercourse with the whites. For example, Governor Aiken owned more than one thousand of them, on his Island of Jehossee, and with the exception of his overseer, his physician, and the Methodist preacher, they seldom saw a white man from one Christmas to another.

Now, these were the fields from which Massachusetts

swelled the numbers of her regiments, with the rank and file, who could not even speak her vernacular. The officers of these regiments may have belonged, and probably did belong, to the "cod fish aristocracy," but all the privates were the genuine Cudjoes and Cuffees of this class – familiarly known as "Gullah negroes."

Their language was an unintelligible jargon to these officers, and nothing short of the "bounty-cash" could have induced them to undertake the drilling of these thick-skulled, semi-savage soldiers.

These garrison commands afforded appropriate training for the richer spoils of the Freedman's Bureau, into which these sell-sacrificing patriots so quickly retired, on the cessation of hostilities; and to which they so tenaciously clung, as long as there was a dollar of congressional appropriation in their treasuries.

CHAPTER THREE

Reconstruction

The first ray of hope that dawned on the dark picture given in the last chapter, was the announcement of President Johnson's "Policy" of restoring the Confederate States to the Union, on their complying with certain conditions precedent. In pursuance of this policy, the Hon. B.F. Perry, a thorough Union man, all before and through the war, but highly respected, and honored by his fellow-citizens for his high character, unswerving integrity, and his honesty of purpose, was appointed "Provisional Governor" by the President. And now, in 1865, for the first time, the forms of government were, once more, assumed.

A convention of the people was called to alter and amend the constitution. Just then began that system of "dirt eating," whereby her own citizens have been made to bring degradation on the State. In complying with the "conditions" emanating from Washington, many of the old land-marks of the past, hallowed by the most sacred associations, were removed by our own people. Those who have felt the power of W.H. Seward, still Secretary of State, at Washington, could easily discern "the hand of Joab" in these requirements, though they came ostensibly from the President. At last, the State, in this fundamental law, was made to abolish slavery – or, rather, to recognize abolition, and to declare that the institution should never again exist within her borders.

Under this constitution, the courts were re-opened, a Legislature elected, as also members of Congress and U.S. Senators. All the conditions were fully complied with, and the State fully equipped for a new departure. Her citizens once more began to breathe freely, and hopes for the future began, at last, to loom up before them.

Unfortunately, all this was soon clouded in impenetrable darkness; and, after a bitter experience of ten long years, no light has yet dawned upon us. In December, 1865, Congress convened in regular session, and, in a very short time, President Johnson's policy was wholly ignored by them, and all his measures and plans were upset by the famous "Reconstruction Acts," by which the State was promptly remanded to her previous condition of "conquered territory." As all the measures already adopted were acceptable to the majority, the forms of government were not absolutely abolished – nor was there any necessity for this. Under the military government, so promptly introduced, the Commanding General was, in fact, the Governor; the orders from headquarters were, in effect, the legislature; the military tribunals were, really, the judiciary; and the Freedman's Bureau was a very acceptable substitute for all municipal authority in cities and towns.

To give some plausible pretext for this over-riding of all the forms of civil government, certain measures were proposed to the legislature for adoption, whereby odium, disfranchisement and public disgrace were to be heaped upon her former leaders, both in the cabinet and in the field. Of course, South Carolina rejected these almost unanimously, failing by a single vote of entire unanimity – and, immediately, a howl of disloyalty was raised against her, from one part of the country to the other. Her sons could not vote for such measures, consistently with their manhood, nor could they have retained any sense of self-respect, had they acquiesced. Their course, in thus resisting these dishonorable and dishonoring requisitions, was anticipated by their political oppressors, and exactly answered their purposes.

Still, these citizens, not yet indoctrinated into the omnip-

otence of the American Congress, were buoyed up by the delu-
sive hope that President Johnson's policy would yet prevail.
They were induced to believe that these Reconstruction Acts
were unconstitutional, and that the executive and judiciary de-
partments of government would yet check the madness of Congress, under the "old flag" which they had resumed. But the President was without a party, and the salaries and tenure of office of
the Supreme Court depended upon the votes of Congress. Not yet
believing all this, they really persuaded themselves that this second "Congressional Reconstruction" would prove a sham. When,
therefore, *another* convention of the State was called under these
Acts, to make *another* constitution, it was regarded merely as a
farce by our wisest and gravest men. None of the *bona fide* citizens of the State took any part whatever in the elections for dele-
gates to this convention, and the scenes enacted at the polls by
the sable voters, were, everywhere, looked upon as exhibitions
for mirth and laughter. But the "farce" went on, however, in
strict conformity to these unprecedented acts; and a convention
was elected, of every hue, and from every clime; from the glossy
blackness of the native African, to the pale-faced Sabbath-school
teacher from Massachusetts – all familiarly known as the "Ring-
streaked and griped," in the slang language of the day.

It was a fatal mistake in thus unanimously holding back
in these, the first elections held under Reconstruction. The pestif-
erous body of "carpet-baggers" were thus permitted to come
boldly to the front, and occupy an open, undisputed field. They
thus had ample room and verge enough for introducing all their
low and despicable, but eminently successful, appliances of party
machinery. The Freedman's Bureau had prepared the way for
them, in their separate church organizations and separate schools,
all of which were soon diverted into the channels of politics.

But their most powerful engine was the "Union-League,"
which bound the unhappy voter hand and foot. By its secret rules
he was not only to vote with unquestioning obedience to party-
dictation, but any effort at independent action on his part would
bring down upon him the wrath and condign punishment of his

own race. Many rites were introduced which appealed directly to his superstitious fears; and the use of the ballot, so new to him, became inextricably entangled with his religion. He was not only taught that it was his truest policy to vote against his former master on every occasion, but a solemn obligation to God, who had emancipated him – always remembering that God had used the Radical party as his chosen instruments for this great end.

This is *now* the fanatical faith of the whole race, and renders them deaf to all appeals and arguments. He was not safe from the vengeance of his own race if he continued outside the League, and once in, his identity was lost, and he became a mere pawn on the political chess-board, to be moved by a higher intelligence. This accounts for the apparent anomaly that, when he gets into straits or troubles, or needs advice about his business, he will come to his former owner with all the humility and confidence of the olden time; he will work for him, and with him, as cheerfully, if not as faithfully, for wages, as he ever did under the former system; but as soon as the subject of politics is broached, he becomes as silent and solemn as a tombstone. *That* is a subject with which "Old Massa" has *nothing* to do; it is sacred between him and his God – but, through the Radical party.

Matters might have been very different, had the whites realized the situation from the first, and while they had the influence over this class, founded on the intercourse, dependence and confidence of long years in the past, they might then have taught their negro fellow-citizens to look upon these vile carpet-baggers as they had been trained to regard the intermeddling abolitionists of former years – as those seeking to subvert all things, and bringing desolation and ruin in their train.

Immediately after the war, there was no animosity between the races. The negroes had behaved admirably during those four long years – when almost all domestic interests had been left mainly to their care and management – and the whites felt grateful to them. The negro was, in no way, responsible for his emancipation, nor was that generation of whites responsible for his past servitude. Both parties had been born under the institution of slavery, and there were no heart-burnings nor feelings of revenge, until these were sown in their hearts by designing scoundrels. If these carpet-baggers had been starved out, as they easily might have been, and the two races left to themselves, there would have been a continuance of that harmony which had resulted from mutual dependence and mutual good will.

But supposing the policy of "fighting the devil with fire" had been thus early adopted, and every one of these votes had been bought up, as might easily have been done. We *now* see that, in the last decade, the State would have saved immensely in money – to say nothing of the prevention of incalculable rascality – even if these votes had been paid, each, twice his assessed value, as recorded in the *ante bellum* tax-books.

To outsiders, it may seem marvellous that so few of these unprincipled carpet-baggers – adventurers, "who left their country for their country's good should so soon and so long *lord* it over a people who had, but recently, filled the world with admiration for their unparalleled military record. The explanation simply is, these miscreants were backed by the whole army and navy of the United States, and these reputed "Rebels" had sworn allegiance to the government, and obedience to all its laws, and constituted authorities.

The government was in the hands of the war-party, who were determined to retain their prodigious power, by every means to which they could resort. These Confederate States had been the backbone of the Democratic party, and this was to be broken, at any and every sacrifice. They could be politically revolutionized by creating a new body of voters, and consolidating them into *their* party ranks. They did not have the constitutional two-thirds majority to effect this fundamental change in the supreme law of the land, therefore these States must be forced to vote for their own degradation. This was done by the opprobrious measures of disfranchising large classes of the whites – enfranchising the whole body of the blacks – and making the adoption of their constitutional amendments a condition precedent to their re-admission into the Union. The slave thus elevated to political equality with his former owner, must be educated and trained for the purposes of the party.

There has always been a dread of the influence of the former master, and this must be overcome by any and every means. Hence, these thick-skinned and heartless, but hungry and zealous partizans, known as carpet-baggers, were the very instruments they needed for this cruel work of sowing suspicion, enmity, and even deadly hate, between the two races. Assured of the protection and unstinted aid from Washington, there was no limit to their unblushing audacity and unscrupulous rapacity. In addition to unlimited military protection, the majority in Congress stood ready to give the forms of law to whatever they required for the good of the party. Is it wonderful that they can so securely and so completely triumph over the natives, bound by obligations the most sacred to passive acquiescence, and then, under the ban of "paroled rebels and traitors"?

There was danger that this cruel policy would alienate the masses at home; and the gain of political strength at the South, be more than counterbalanced by the defection and disgust of friends at the North. Hence, the necessity, from time to time, to "fire the Northern heart," and rekindle the hate generated by four years of bloody strife. This was effected by encouraging the carpet-baggers to fresh provocations, more aggravating than human nature could bear, and then to magnify any effort at resistance, or any natural expression of indignation into "Southern outrages" and "Southern disloyalty," to be heralded from one end of the Union to the other. The Southern newspapers had but a limited and local circulation, and the press was arrayed against them, with slim opportunities for either explanation or correction.

South Carolina was particularly odious as the leader in Secession. Whatever justification or appeal came from her borders fell on ears most unsympathizing, and the stereotyped reply, "served her right!" was the only satisfaction vouchsafed. Her slaves were in a vast majority, more than three to two in the aggregate, and in some sections of her low country, as many as ten to one. The Congressional policy of reconstruction, therefore, has not only revolutionized her government and closed her record as one of the "old thirteen," but has changed her caste among the peoples of the earth, as far as legislation can do so. A native from the wilds of Africa could, at that time, have reached higher stations, and enjoyed greater privileges and immunities, than any of her native-born sons of the great Anglo-Saxon family.

It was in circumstances such as these, that this hybrid Constitutional Convention selected R. K. Scott as their standard-bearer.

Several of our thinking men, more far-seeing than others, began to realize that this abnormal state of things might become permanent, and, by their advice, a counter organization was attempted in this the first election of State officers, under the new constitution, in 1868. Public meetings were held in various parts of the State, and, at first, these were largely attended by the colored voters. Notably, in Columbia, Gen. Wade Hampton, efficiently aided by Col. J. P. Thomas, was earnest in his addresses and appeals. He had been the first leading citizen to urge that the ballot should be given to the freedmen, and was buoyed by the hope that they could be taught to use it properly. Several of the colored leaders came out boldly on his side and even made speeches echoing his noble sentiments. But our politicians were too much hampered by their old fashioned notions of honesty and fair-dealing, to contend with the unscrupulous and well-disciplined hosts opposed to them.

While our men were relying upon argument, old associations, and moral suasion, all these were as nothing when compared with the all-powerful greenback. Those funds, subscribed by the office-holders under the government as "beneficiaries of the Republican Party," came flowing freely into the pockets of these ebony orators, and instantly charmed their tongues into silence.

Beverly Nash, subsequently the Radical Senator from Richland, *then* thought $500 a vast sum – enough, at any rate, to cause him to turn his back very suddenly on his friends of lang syne. His example was followed, whenever the same experiment was made.

Our people, however, went through the form of calling a Party Convention, and nominated a full State ticket. The Hon. W. D. Porter, of Charleston, than whom no civilian stood higher in public estimation for all the qualities which mark the statesman and the patriot, was selected a candidate for Governor.

The canvass was a spasmodic affair; as, contending on the rostrum with those who had so recently been their slaves, was no very pleasant inducement to our speakers. When the election came off, Mr. Porter was beaten by R. K. Scott, by precisely the same majority that crowned J. K. Jilison as victor over the humble writer of these pages for the office of "Superintendent of Education" – a clear *two to one/*

This Jilison was another of those self-sacrificing philanthropists, who had recently left some New England home (?) on a mission to this stricken State, that around her sick bed he might watch and *prey.*

It was Scott's experience, as the head of the Freedman's Bureau, which had recommended him to his party; as the eyes of the whole hungry crew were fixed upon the Treasury, and he was known to have become expert in diverting public funds. His financial operations are out of the line of this little book, and the reader should congratulate himself on this. He then inaugurated measures which have since made this Treasury a charnel house of fraud, crime and corruption, whose exploration would become equally disgusting to reader and to writer.[1] His lead has been so persistently followed by his successors, that it has actually become stench in the nostrils of the harpies themselves, and we have heard cries for burlesque "Reform" even from their own ranks.

During Scott's first term, the whites, for the most part, still persisted in the stand-off policy, hoping for relief from the United States Supreme Court. He thus had an open field for the inauguration of all his measures. But, as these developed more fully, and the prospect of relief grew more and more faint, the Democratic

---

1. See Appendix – *passim.*

party became sufficiently aroused to organize "Clubs" all over the State, and to adopt the policy of conciliation.

They, therefore, in Party Convention assembled, prepared a platform low enough, and broad enough, for any one of conservative principles to mount, whatever might have been his "race, color, or previous condition of servitude." They nominated for Governor, Judge Carpenter, at that time the least objectionable of the carpet-bag fraternity; and opened the campaign against Scott and Company, under the name of the "Reform Party." The most earnest efforts were made to break the ranks of the opposing hosts. The whole summer was given up to speechmaking and the usual electioneering tactics; but the result showed that it was too late! Notwithstanding some seeming defection at first, when it came to the test of the ballot-box, the colored voters went solidly for their political masters, and by an increased majority, showed how effectual had been the training already described.

The Radical leaders were, at first, very much alarmed at this policy of selecting leaders from their ranks. It would be a moral absurdity to allude to anything like conscience in their case, but vice instinctively cowers before virtue, and even "devils believe and *tremble.*" Some new machinery must be brought to bear against this threatened danger, and the peculiar military genius of Scott now found a wide field for operation.

Under his inspiration the Legislature organized a "State Constabulary Force," having its headquarters in Columbia, in charge of a Chief Constable. This tool had the power of appointing as many deputies as he wished, and wherever it pleased him; with a squad of detectives and hungry mischief-makers always under their command, and in the pay of the State, through a profligate fee-bill.

On warrants issued from some magistrate's office in Columbia, generally based on the affidavit of the Chief Constable himself, these had power to arrest any citizen in *any* county of the State, and hale him to the jail in Columbia. This was in close imitation of those nice little garrisons which had proved such effectual supports and constant feeders to the Freedman's Bureau.

In both, the main object was to foment, instead of quelling disturbances; the *fines* having been the inducements in the older system, and the *fees* proved equally efficacious in the new, in promoting active service in these vagrant constables. The proceeding was very simple for the initiatory warrant. The deputy reported some name to the chief, who immediately made oath before some pliant magistrate, "that he had good reason to believe," etc., and, forthwith, the irresistible warrant was issued. The obvious aim in both institutions was to engender and foster ill will and bad blood between the races.

The next grand stroke of military policy was the passage of the militia law under the same inspiration, giving the Governor, through his ready Adjutant-General (F. J. Moses), the privilege of rejecting any company organized under its liberal provisions. It is needless to say, that every company of whites was promptly rejected on the ground of disloyalty, and only colored companies and regiments were received.

But, the crowning enormity in this whole series of tyrannical usurpations, was the purchasing and issuing improved small arms, with an unlimited supply of fixed ammunition, to all the colored regiments throughout the State.

It required no prophet to foretell the deplorable results of such a reckless policy as this. To arm and equip the colored race, exclusively – constituting, as they did, so large a majority throughout the State, and, but a few years before, an ignorant and debased mob of emancipated slaves – could only be accounted for by turning to the desperate character of these leaders themselves, whose well-known policy was to "rule or ruin," or rather to ruin and rule.

In the middle and lower counties, where the Radical majorities were well assured, this game of organizing and arming the negroes, was played without serious consequences. As there was no object to be gained, in these counties, by supplementing the militia with the infamous constabulary force, this "playing sogers" was rather a source of amusement, and would have been enjoyed as such, had it not caused serious interruption to their plantation work, by their too frequent drilling and parading. Besides, it was embarrassing to set Col. Sambo and Maj. Cuffee to ditching the rice-fields, up to their middles in mud and water – a work only suitable for high privates. But it was desirable to these leaders to have them tickled with a sense of their importance and privileges as citizen-soldiers; and these organizations might be substituted for the Union Leagues, now beginning to flag in interest.

But in the upper and border counties, where the whites had a majority, or were so nearly equal as to make the result of a contest doubtful, the whole force of this party machinery, in both its branches, was brought to bear, with very memorable results.

Here the constabulary force flourished in full blast, and all their professional ingenuity was called into play to produce sensations, and to cause troubles the most serious. The militia companies were very much under their influence, and were drilled in other tactics beside the military.

To secure accuracy in the details in the working of these military and judicial devices, the writer will confine himself, in the next few chapters, to what occurred in the County of Laurens alone, during the political campaigns of 1870 and 1872.

CHAPTER FOUR

☆ ☆ ☆ ☆

Reconstruction in Laurens County

The year 1870 will long be remembered by the citizens of Laurens County. Here it was doubtful how the contest between the Democratic, or "Reform" party, and the Radicals would result in the then approaching elections for State officers. The Democrats had carried the county two years before, but the Radicals claimed that they had not been fully organized at that time, and that the colored votes, in fact, outnumbered the whites.

It, therefore, presented a fair field for the introduction and manipulation of all their party contrivances, and the excitement soon became intense.

It becomes necessary, at the very outset, to make the reader acquainted with the recognized leader of the Radical party, in this county, and at that time. And among the many humiliations to which we have been subjected under reconstruction, it is not the least to be forced, not only to notice, but to give prominence to such vile characters as Joe Crews. But, as he was the type of a large class, who really became the leaders in these, the Dark Ages in South Carolina, the reader must consent to a rather familiar acquaintance with him, in this local narrative.

Before the war, he was a low "negro-trader," making his bread by trafficking in negroes, and with negroes. In their most debased condition their nature was congenial with his own, and he so fully understood and appreciated their peculiar characteristics, that he found no difficulty in becoming their recognized leader in their changed condition; and in making more money out of them, and by means of their votes, than he ever did before the war. His availability was soon recognized in Columbia, and we shortly find him a "member of the Legislature," a "Commissioner of Elections," a "Military Aid" to the redoubtable Scott, a "Trial Justice," and a general dispenser of all the local offices within the gift of the Governor. In Columbia, he was generally distinguished as among the scavengers of the carpetbag government – always a ready tool to do their "dirty work," – which office he found to be no sinecure.

As leader of the party in Laurens, he was entrusted with full powers to organize the militia, and to conduct the campaign according to his own notions, which were known to be unscrupulous enough. He soon had his companies filled up – some six or seven hundred stand of improved Springfield rifles issued – with any amount of fixed ammunition with them.

A complete programme of military barbecues was arranged for the summer, always to be attended, armed and equipped, as the (party) law directed.

It was his harranguing at these barbecues that first fired the colored heart. Some of his speeches were listened to by respectable citizens, who testified in the public prints of the day, and over their own signatures, to his highly incendiary diatribes. Among very many other things, he advised the laborers, now that they had arms in their hands, to seize whatever of the crops they thought they ought to have, and if any fuss was made, they could easily burn them out, as matches were cheap. That *they* now had the power, and the white man must be taught to know his place.

Under such teachings as these, it was not to be wondered at, that companies of colored militia, in going to, and returning from these gatherings, with arms in their hands, should be insolent, and sometimes even violent towards their former owners. There were many instances of insults offered to ladies, while riding in their carriages over the public roads; and of indignities the most gross, perpetrated by them, on the premises of some obnoxious farmers.

All this may have been foreseen, and probably was foreseen by these leaders; but what cared they for law or peace, if they could only secure the votes? What cared they for the restiveness and indignation of the white man, who, himself disarmed, was thus forced to witness the marching and counter-marching of his former slaves about his premises; these being assured too, that they could trample upon all law, with impunity? These leaders knew that there was no tribunal, State or Federal, to which he could appeal, with any hope of relief; and if he attempted to redress his own wrongs, this would be made to play directly into their own hands.

These military annoyances, however, were only spasmodic, and there were intervals of relief. But the other nuisance of the "constabulary," was a constant running sore. These, too, were under the control of the omnivorous Joe, and were to be at his beck and call every hour of the day and night too. There were some half-dozen of them in and about his armory, on the courthouse square, and were the lowest of the low. Representing many nationalities, they had been combed out of the purlieus of cities, where vice is a profession, and crime their education. Ostensibly the conservators of the peace, they were in fact, the instigators in all mischief-making, whether military or rowdy. Even these had their sub-agents, like themselves, on public pay, and known only to themselves. By these a constant espionage was kept up, embracing even the house-servants on their list, by whom all unguarded expressions around one's own fire-side, and in the sanctity of the domestic circle, were promptly reported to headquarters, often with variations and exaggerations.

Superadded to all these, and as a backbone to the whole infamous structure, a company of United States troops was stationed near the town, brought there, Joe said, by *his* influence at Washington.

With all these means and appliances, and actuated by a deadly hate against his own race, who had, long since, refused him all social intercourse, or even recognition, Joe Crews kept the community in a constant state of excitement and irritation, which only required a spark to develop into a popular outbreak.

The day of election, October 19th, 1870, was looked forward to with great apprehension. The armory was in a large vacant store, just in front of the court-house building, and in this were several hundred rifles, ready for use. At Crews' own house, some quarter of a mile distant, his barn had been converted into a temporary armory, ditches were dug on the inside along the four walls, and loop-holes cut very low, so that the besieged might stand in the ditch and fire, with the least exposure!

He also had, as Commissioner of Elections, ordered all the boxes to be brought to town, and opened, one in each corner of the public square. Heretofore, they had been distributed over the county, at convenient distances for the voters, in the several precincts; but, for more reasons than one, he wanted them all together. One was, that the little game of *repeating* could very conveniently and safely be played, where it was next to impossible to distinguish his voters, either by names or features; and another was, that, in case of an outbreak, it would be best to have his forces "well in hand."

All the preparations were clearly known to both friend and foe, long before the day of election. Of course, the whites adopted some plan of counter-organization, for self-defence. They would have been less than men, if they had left their family-hearths, and their wives and children, exposed to all manner of violence and insult, without some scheme for mutual protection. This was done, in the first place, by purchasing arms. Several merchants of the village sent on orders for cases of Winchester rifles, which were opened and distributed in the broad light of day. In the next place, certain experienced and prudent citizens were designated to take command, and give all necessary orders, in case of actual colli- sion. These were appointed by the Democratic Club, a party organization, at that time common all over the State. And, just here, the writer of these pages can assert, without fear of success- ful contradiction, that there never has been a Ku-Klux organization in the county of Laurens, either before, during, or since the riot of 1870. This fact was so notorious, that when certain citizens of this county were brought to trial in the United States Circuit Court, on a charge of *"conspiracy* and murder," no effort was made on the part of the prosecution to prove the existence of a single Ku-Klux Klan. They had an inexhaustible number of false witnesses, ready to establish any fact, on oath, for a consideration; but even Crews himself was ashamed of this lie.

The election day at length came on. Early in the morning, the court-house square was literally covered with a perfect black sea of colored voters. The boxes were all opened, but for hours after the voting began, all access to any of them was physically impossible to any but the party. The managers were all Radicals, and the whites soon saw that all contest was hopeless. By thus giving them the field, the morning passed off quietly enough.

In the afternoon, a runner brought the news, that the negroes were arming in Crews' premises. This was promptly announced to Col. Smith, the gentlemanly officer in command of the United States garrison, and he was soon seen wending his way to the scene of action, unaccompanied even by an orderly. Arriving there, he did see some twenty or thirty of them in line, with arms in their hands. In answer to his question, as to what they were after, with that tact and promptness at lying so characteristic of the race, in every condition, they said: "We only funnin; we got through votin, and thought we would have a little fun in drillin for a little while." The Colonel then peremptorily ordered them, if they had got through voting, to put those arms just where they had found them, and go directly home. With the same promptness with which they used to heed their owners, in days of yore, they quietly deposited the arms in the barn, and as quietly took the road from the village. With this little interlude, the day passed off with less confusion than usually attends a sales day.

The Circuit Court, then in session, had adjourned over the day of election; the Female College also closed for the day, and some of the merchants had suspended business. Col. Smith, of the garrison, who had had marching orders for several days previous, remained at his post until the election was over. That very night, however, he struck his tents, and took up his line of march for Newberry. *All* parties believed now that all danger was over. The next day the Court resumed its sessions – Judge Vernon presiding – the young ladies once more walked, fearlessly, through the streets in going to the college, and business everywhere was resumed – every one breathing more freely. A goodly number of negroes came in from the country to "receive their rewards," but by no means the crowd of the day before. The whites were also in greatly reduced numbers – not more present than usual on court weeks. Everything went on quietly and peacefully until eleven o'clock.

There have been many conflicting statements as to the origin of the "Riot of the 20th October," but the following is the account of a respectable eye-witness, given, too, under the sanction of an oath. A citizen I and one of the constabulary had a personal difficulty, which resulted in a fist-fight. This was near the armory, in and around which was quite a crowd of the leading negroes of the campaign. A friend of the citizen, pistol in hand, went up to the scene of the fight, to see fair play, as he said. Seeing that his friend had got the best of the fight, he was about to return his pistol to its case – under his coat, and attached to a belt behind – when it was accidentally discharged. A cry was immediately heard among the negroes, "They are firing upon us!" and, together, they all disappeared in the armory. Soon guns were seen protruding from the windows upstairs, in the direction of the public square, immediately in front; and a volley of some twenty guns was fired.

There was quite a sprinkling of men on the square, and yet "nobody was hurt." This is easily accounted for. These bold militiamen thought their only agency was in "cocking the gun and pulling the trigger," and that the blood-thirsty bullet would itself seek its victim independently of all aim.

The effect of the volley on the scattered crowd was startling enough. A hornet's nest suddenly turned over, could not have produced more flying to and fro, or more rage and venom among the assailed. Some ran for their arms – secreted near by, the day before, in case of an emergency – shot-guns from the show-cases, were seized and loaded on the double-quick; others with no arms at all but walking canes and brick-bats – all rushed madly for the front door and windows of the armory. These yielded readily to the furious onset of the whites, and similar openings in the rear opened as readily to the mad outset of the blacks. It was no fight at all; for as soon as these sable warriors saw the determined rush for their stronghold, they instantly dropped their sixteen-shooters on the floor, made a break for the back windows and doors, and this eye-witness avers that they made the quickest time on record down the declivity in the rear. It seems that some of our boys who had served from Bull Run to Appomattox could not resist the temptation for some sharp-shooting at a flying foe; but they declared that a black target, changing its level every second so amazingly, afforded them a poor chance to show their skill. There was only one struck fatally on the retreat, and he lingered for several days. Two others, shot in the building, made up all the casualties of this famous affair.

It sounds rather tame, after the sensational articles published by telegraph and otherwise throughout the length and breadth of the Union, and with the imposing captions of "Outrages in Laurens County," "War of Races Begun," "Rebellion still Rampant," etc., etc., to come down to the truth of history, and chronicle the simple tale. But the foregoing account *is* true; and it *was* merely an election row, growing out of an accidental street fight; and, that three lives were lost. The whole affair, from the firing of the pistol to the discharge of the last gun, did not occupy more than fifteen minutes. If the same row had occurred anywhere else outside of a Reconstructed State, it would not have excited any attention beyond the community directly interested.

The conflict, though "sharp" and "short," was equally "decisive." The colored population had suddenly disappeared, and as effectually as though the earth had opened and swallowed man, woman and child of the race; for none of them, of any age or of either sex, were seen on the streets for the rest of that day.

Old Laurens could boast of *one* day, at least, under a white man's government.

The arms stowed in the armory were now in the hands of the captors; and they were disposed to hold them, as there were flying rumors of "rallying in the country," and many other sensational items, so usual in times of great excitement. Armory No. 2, at the barn, was still intact. In case of a surprise from the country, this post would afford much aid and comfort to an attacking force; but everything had become so quiet, that there was no excuse for forcible seizures. It was wisely advised and decided to carry out the balance of the day's campaign as law-abiding citizens.

As before remarked, the Circuit Court was then in session, and at the firing of the guns, the building was soon left to the sole occupancy of the Judge and the Clerk. After peace was so suddenly conquered, its business was resumed, at least, so far as to hear the presentment of the grand jury on the disturbance of the peace then transpiring. This was an able and truthful paper, and traced the developments to their true source. They advised that the Court should take cognizance of the disturbance of the public peace, and, to prevent further complications, itself to take possession of the public arms. In pursuance of this recommendation, Judge Vernon ordered the Sheriff to take into his custody the arms then in the hands of the citizens and with his posse to remove those then stored in Crews' barn, to a place of safety. All this was carried out at once; and, in a short time the sheriff had the arms stored away in his office, under the Court-room, and an efficient guard placed over them. Thus, before night closed in, matters seemed to have calmed down completely.

At that critical time, Laurens had an imposing illustration of the triumphs of "rumor," so graphically described by Virgil, in periods of great excitement. In an incredibly short interval of time, the news had spread to every point of the compass, that the "fight" was actually going on at the town; and the casualties and other incidents were multiplied and exaggerated in proportion to the distance from the scene of action. Of course there were "mount-ings in hot haste;" and, during all the afternoon and night, squads of mounted men, all armed, could be seen riding into town, with no ordinary speed. It would naturally be expected, that while these excited bodies of horsemen were meeting with fugitives running out of town, some serious collisions would have occurred. But, strange to say, nothing of the kind took place in the daytime. And, as to the number of these armed men thus assembled, there has been much exaggeration. It is true that the instinct of race, brought together many bold and determined spirits, but these were mainly from the adjoining counties. Those in the vicinity, not knowing whence the rumored "rally" might come, yielded to the higher instinct of home protection. It can safely be asserted, that no time after the row, were there more than three hundred non-residents in the town, at one and the same time. Most of these, as soon as they saw that their services were not needed, quietly turned their horses' heads the way they had come.

It would be very gratifying to the writer, if the narrative of the proceedings of this affair could close with the day. On a calm review, after an interval of more than five years, no impartial and intelligent lover of his country, who is cognizant of all the antecedents and circumstances of that day, can blame the citizens of Laurens, for what then and there took place. What has been so often paraded before the country as "a bloody and outrageous riot," was simply the disarming an ignorant and lawless mob, when they had given the clearest evidence that they were bent on mischief the most serious, and this, too, either in actual self-defence, or in obedience to an order of Court.

But the truth of history requires that some of the proceedings of that night should also be chronicled; simply premising that none have more earnestly condemned these outrages, than the citizens of Laurens themselves, in comparison with whom these ruffians are the merest handful. There is no evidence that they even belonged to the county, and even if they did, what county is there, North, South, East or West, which cannot furnish rowdies enough to perpetrate all that was done in Laurens, at a time, too, of excitement the most intense?

The morning after the riot, the whole town was thrown into confusion, and all were much shocked at the rumors of these outrages. They were much magnified at first, but finally subsided into four distinct cases, each of which was carefully examined into by the jury of inquest.

One party had taken an obnoxious negro from a cabin where he had taken refuge, and so maltreated him that he died a few days after.

The body of another negro was found, stark and stiff, on the side of the public road, with no indications to show the manner of his death.

One Powell, a carpet-bagger, and just voted for as Judge of Probate, was found on the public road, near Milam's Trestle, with several bullet-holes through his head and body; and, by his side, the body of a negro man, also murdered as brutally as himself.

Near Martin's Depot, also on the public road, the body of Wade Perrin, negro member of the Legislature, was found, pierced with one or more bullet-holes.

These three last mentioned outrages were perpetrated on the public road, running along the track of the old Laurens Railroad, and might have been the work of one and the same party. The most distant was Perrin, some fifteen miles from the village; the single negro being found near Clinton, about nine miles off, and Powell and his companion not more than four miles.

The case first mentioned was three or four miles from town, but in a different direction from all the others.

The commonly received opinion, or surmise, was that the three last mentioned casts were the brutal work of one and the same party of desperadoes, who were really out in search of Crews. That, maddened by the events of the day, and the whisky of the night, to say nothing of "the instigations of the devil," they wantonly and brutally murdered those of the same party whom they chanced to meet.

Whoever they may have been, by their diabolical work,

they disgusted and horrified those they pretended to befriend, even more than those who were distant and disinterested. The whole community regarded these horrible acts not only as repugnant to our institutions and the civilization of the age, but as against the instincts of a common humanity, barbarous or civilized, heathen or Christian.

CHAPTER FIVE

☆ ☆ ☆ ☆

Joe Crews

The reader will naturally, ask, what became of Joe Crews in these exciting scenes? Surely, this military aid to the Governor, or rather his Lieutenant-Governor, as far as Laurens was concerned, must have had a prominent place in the picture. He who had made so many speeches, threatening carnage and blood, would now, certainly, come to the front, sweep the "white trash" out of his way, and thus unify his dominions.

Alas for him, the truth of history must be told! He was on the ground, he heard the reports of his costly rifles, and he rushed – but it was *the other way*.

His escape gives the lie to any charge of "conspiracy," in bringing on the "riot." Had there been any thing of the kind, *his* fate would have been fixed at the very outset. On the contrary, he was allowed to run from the scene unnoticed; the attention of all being fixed on the real point of danger – the armory.

He afterwards published an account of his escape in a Columbia newspaper, telling how he secreted himself in a large hollow log in the immediate vicinity of the town; how he was fed there for three days and nights, and how he was kept constantly informed of all that was going on. That within the three days, limited by law, he had opened and counted the ballot boxes, which had been safely brought to him from his house, and had

59

taken the result of the count safely to Columbia.

What a picture is here presented to the imagination of the patriot! Remember, we were, at this time, approaching the first "Centennial of American Independence," and that this scene is laid near the heart of South Carolina, one of the "old thirteen." That the cardinal principle established by this "independence," is the sovereignty of the people.

But let us creep up to that little copse of wood, and what do we see? There, at the mouth of a large hollow log, where his own conduct had driven him for refuge from an outraged people; sits this old degraded negro trader, with the suffrages of some three thousand of the "sovereign people," sealed, in several boxes, before him. He is, at one and the same time, a candidate for the votes of these people, and sole Commissioner of Elections to take charge of them. He was, a day or two before, the chief manipulator of these voters themselves, and now had the sole right to count out the votes and record the result. His managers of elections who should have assisted him, had all fled to parts unknown; but he was equal to the occasion. Not wishing to be troubled with handling so many small bits of paper, he pulls out of his side pocket a greasy memorandum book, writes down a few figures to satisfy his congenial "powers that be," and the work is done! The political fate of a whole county is thus fixed for two years to come. Can Dahomey or even Louisiana exceed this in *broad farce?*

Joe did not let the public know how he got *out* of the county, but Capt. Estes, of the United States Infantry, gave all the particulars to the writer of this narrative.

Capt. Estes had reached Laurens with a small garrison, the fourth day after the riot, and had taken quarters for himself and men in the abandoned depot of the Laurens Railroad. On Sunday night, October 30th, Joe presented himself at head-quarters, and demanded protection from the United States forces, and safe transportation beyond the limits of Laurens County. Joe was looking very seedy and haggard, and the Captain's sympathy was soon enlisted. He told him to return about five o'clock in the morning; and, if he would implicitly obey all orders, he would soon take him to a place of safety. Joe came, long before the hour fixed, and rendered himself so disgusting by his boasts and threats, that the captain determined to have a little innocent revenge.

The conveyance was to be a square-bodied handcar, and the passengers, all told – two men at the crank, two armed soldiers, one on each side of the captain; and Joe was to be wrapped in canvas and deposited in the bottom of the car, to represent a quarter of beef. This arrangement was literally carried out; and they had not proceeded many miles before sounds of distress were heard from the canvas. In answer to his inquiry, Joe told the captain he would certainly die, if he continued to breathe the same air much longer. Estes reminded him of his promise, and assured him that he would no longer be responsible for his safety, if he ventured even to cut the sack. As the sounds of distress still continued, the captain cut a small slit just where his mouth was, and gave him partial relief.

With this small supply of oxygen, Joe began again to swagger, though Lying in sackcloth and red clay. But the captain could easily silence him by asking his men if they did not notice some suspicious-looking groups of men, apparently watching them from a distance. This would so stir Joe's blood, that the oxygen would not serve the increased circulation, and sounds of distress were again mumbled through the crevice.

Sometimes the captain would order a sudden halt, and, while he whispered to his men that he believed the enemy was about to rush upon them, he declared he could hear Joe's heart beating distinctly. After one of these sudden halts, they all left the car, with Joe lying there alone, and, after a few minutes, the captain heard a feeble call from the car. Upon his assuring Joe that there was no immediate danger, and that they had only stopped to pick a few *blackberries*, Joe actually arose to a sitting position, with the exclamation, "D—n your blackberries, when a man's life is in danger." The captain simply ordered him *down* again, with the alternative of desertion to his fate; and instantly

Joe was again metamorphosed into a quarter of beef. The captain avers that he could see traces of perspiration even through the sack, and really expected to find his braggadocio spirit completely wilted, after thirty odd miles of such experience.

He was greatly mistaken, however; for, no sooner was Joe fairly on his feet once more, than he began to harangue listening groups of admirers at his landing place, in Newberry, in a strain that ancient Pistol might have envied. Pistol when relieved of the presence of the infuriated Welshman, whose leek he had just been forced to eat, cried out, "All hell shall stir for this!" Joe was for stirring up the whole army and navy of the United States – a threat more terrible to *his* audience. Pistol could show a "bloody cockscomb," as some excuse for his blustering, while Joe's skin was wholly intact, though saturated in every part with sweat and moisture.

Such was the exit of this famous "Colonel of Militia;" and it may be added, that his face was not again seen in Laurens County for more than two years afterwards.

The little irregularity in the counting of the ballots could easily be slurred over, in Columbia, as his returns were to be made to those of the same political family. The pretended counting *must* have been done by Crews alone, as all the managers were scattered to the four winds, and the boxes were left at his house. Even his infamous coadjutor, "the Hon. Senator Owens," had made his exit, and shed *his* perspiration, under a load of wheat-straw, in a wagon bound for Greenville. This was an aristocratic method of transportation, as most of the others felt constrained to burrow all the day-time, and only sneak softly away at night, like other beasts of prey.

Nothing has heretofore been said of this Owens, mainly because he always seemed to give the lead to Joe, and one such character is enough for one book. But those who knew them both, among their appropriate associates, regarded Owens as the meaner of the two. They contrast them somewhat in the following manner:

Joe had audacity; Owens is a sneak! Joe was the highwayman, who, when his victims were all disarmed, could breathe forth great swelling words; Owens is the assassin, who deals the deadly blow from behind, and slinks off into the darkness of night. "To give the devil his due," Joe has been known to perform some acts of real kindness, and even of charity; but, from universal testimony, no such sentiments "have ever approached the head or heart" of Owens. Joe made no pretensions; Owens can be a genuine Uriah Heape, in humility, while talking to such white men as can stomach him. From statements made by those who ought to know him best in Columbia, he was more malignant and fiendish against those of his own race, in the Laurens troubles, than Joe ever was, and was really responsible, for most of the outrageous treatment of innocent citizens, though he managed to keep "behind the curtains" all the time. As to their war record, Joe stayed at home and cheated on a private scale; Owens deserted to the enemy, early in the war, and cheated both the army and Confederacy.

It is a disgusting task to unearth so vile a character as this of Owens, from the sinks and sewers of his moral prostitution; and, for the future, the reader is assured, that his memory will be left there to rot, as far as this narrative is concerned. The mortifying part of the task is to confess, that the leprosy of his example has tainted others, who were weak in principle, but strong in covetousness. They saw that, in his case –

> Plait sin in gold,
> And the strong lance of Justice,
> hurtless, breaks.

And they soon yearned for the same kind of armor. 'Tis true, they soon found that they had to stoop lower, and delve deeper in pollution than they ever dreamed of; but what miner, when fairly under ground, regards such sacrifices, when blinded by the prospect of the shining reward?

Still more mortifying is it to confess, that most of these, both leaders and followers, are native South Carolinians. The consoling thought is, that this base apostacy is confined to no period nor clime. "In the days of innocency," even in the contracted garden, planted by God himself, the beguiling serpent was found, a ready tool for the "father of lies;" and in these degenerate times, in the midst of demoralization and misrule, is it to wondered at that he is rather the tempted than the tempter? We can only the more admire that manhood and integrity, landmarks of a former civilization, which, in the midst of wrecked fortunes and blasted hopes, can add fresh dignity to words long familiar, but never so fully felt before – "All is lost, save honor!"

The friends of Joe Crews (if he had any) must excuse the writer for sometimes designating him as "Joe" and sometimes as "Crews." The fact is, like Napoleon Bonaparte, he had distinguished both names, and was as well known by the one as by the other. At the time of which we are writing his influence seemed realty potential with the motley crew who were managing the ship of State; and some of his statements, personal to the writer, have reached even beyond their filthy purlieus, and, in this connection, seem to call for some notice on his part. If this serves no other purpose, it will, at least, show the license of these times, when fabrications the most monstrous could be established by any amount of "legal" but venal evidence; and will also illustrate Joe's accuracy and ingenuity in reporting facts, and in making charges.

The Female College is next door to the residence of Mrs. Crews; and sometime after the row was over, it was reported to the president that Mrs. C. was in her porch, surrounded by her children, and that they all seemed to be in great distress. He at once went over, and invited her to come over to the College with her family, if they felt uneasy where they were, and he would give them the same protection he was able to give his own family. Mrs. C. thanked him cordially, but remarked that, as she had never done any harm in the town, she did not believe that any one would injure either herself or her children. The president confirmed her in this opinion, and returned to his own home.

Now, the version given by Joe is, that Maj. Leland, President of Laurens Female College, deliberately resorted to this device to get the family out of the house in order that it might be robbed, or burned, or both!

A little later in the day, when the sheriff's "posse" was drawn up in line in front of Mrs. C.'s house, waiting for the wagons to come for the arms stored in the barn-armory, this same gentlemen was standing near the gate as a spectator. The officer in command of the "posse," requested him to step up to the house, and assure Mrs. C. that neither her front nor back yard would be trespassed upon, as the only object of the visit was the barn, which was separated from the front yard by a wide lane. In complying with this request, Mrs. C. handed him a bright-barrelled Springfield rifle, requesting him to take it, as it belonged to the State, and had been left there a day or two before, by an old colored man. He at first declined to take anything from the house, but as she insisted that it would be a relief to her if he would do so, he brought it as far as the gate. There he met the Rev. Mr. Kisler, and jocularly remarking that *his* would be the safest hands for such a piece, he handed it to him. In justice to Mr. K., it should be remarked, that he was seen to deposit the gun in the first of the wagons that arrived.

Joe's version of this is, that Maj. L. visited Mrs. C.'s house a second time, and at night, and took therefrom a pet fowling-piece of his, valued at seventy-five dollars, notwithstanding the entreaties and pleas of Mrs. C. to the contrary.

These misrepresentations of his motives and conduct, did not strike the party aimed at very pleasantly.

He was complaining of them once in the presence of a pious, but pleasantly sarcastic lady friend, who remarked that he deserved this treatment for *flying* directly in the face of a plain injunction of scripture. In vain did he search his memory for any text condemning kindness and charity; and, on calling triumphantly for one, he was silenced by the reply, "Did not our Saviour Himself say, 'cast not your pearls before swine, lest they trample them under foot, and turn again and rend you'?"

There were other fabrications of Joe's which are too absurd to be recorded. But to those of us who resided in Laurens,

in those dark days, they loomed up in very threatening proportions, when we knew with what facility, any charge, however
absurd and ridiculous could be substantiated by any number of
sworn witnesses. In fact, the charge on which the writer *was*
finally arrested and imprisoned for five long weeks, did not have
even the semblance of foundation which might be claimed for
these.

CHAPTER SIX

☆ ☆ ☆ ☆

Laurens – After the Riot

The old adage, that after a storm comes a calm, was not verified very promptly in Laurens. For days and weeks, after the events recorded in a previous chapter, the public mind was kept at fever heat of excitement. Rumors of parties organized to burn the town at night, and other diabolical schemes of the scattered leaders, were well calculated to cause continued apprehension and anxiety. Patrols were detailed to watch every night, and in every part of the corporate limits, and every head of a family was expected to guard his own premises. Then came a rumor that Gov. Scott had decided to send a regiment of his colored militia to garrison the county. There *was* some truth in this, but the prompt and spirited *veto* of the whites in Columbia, soon made him abandon the scheme. Then there were other rumors of the immediate proclamation of martial law by the President, and of wholesale arrests by United States Marshals, which produced wide-spread consternation and alarm. No one on retiring to bed at night, had any assurance that he would be found there the next morning.

In fact, this state of uncertainty and uneasiness would have become intolerable, if long continued. But gradually these rumors subsided by their own limitations. It was found that these leaders were more effectually demoralized than was at first supposed; and that they were more engaged in securing their own safety, than in plotting mischief against others.

Scott found that there was a spirit aroused over the whole State, from the unblushing abuse of the ballot-box in the recent election, with which it would be dangerous to tamper, and was disposed to remain quiet enough. As to the United States authorities, they had so often been deceived by the "cry of wolf" from these same parties, that they contented themselves with sending a small garrison, with officers competent to inquire into the matters for themselves.

There were still two fruitful sources of trouble and annoyance; and as long as these continued, there could be no hope of lasting peace and quiet. These were the "public arms," and the "State constabulary force." It is true that most of these arms were in the custody of the sheriff; but very many more were in the hands of the colored militia, issued to them before the riot; and our friends in the country felt no little anxiety on this account.

As for the constabulary force, they began to appear, one after another, and to give every indication of resuming their former practices.

In view of these facts, the citizens of Laurens appointed a committee of three, to wait on the Governer, in Columbia, make a report of these public nuisances, and to urge upon him to remove or abate them if possible. The citizens selected the three *they* thought above all suspicion of complicity with rowdyism, viz: Dr. J. W. Simpson, the patriarch of the town, S. R. Todd, Sr., the oldest and most substantial merchant of the place, and J. A. Leland, President of the Female College. Capt. Estes, of the United States garrison, kindly consented to accompany this committee to Columbia, mainly to testify to the readiness with which the whites had given up, and were still willing to deliver to the proper authority all the public arms in their possession. He was also willing to assure the Governor that, while a United States Marshal alone, or accompanied by one or more United States soldiers, could ride through the length and breadth of the county with perfect impunity, whether by day or night, his constabulary were forced to prowl about like wolves, with about the same chance of safety if detected in indulging *their* instincts.

Through the kind offices of Captain Estes, an interview with the committee was accorded by Scott the very night of their arrival, and in his own parlor.

Dr. Simpson, the chairman, read to him a carefully prepared paper, tracing the recent disturbances to the unfortunate arming of the militia, and the mischievous intermeddling and reckless course of the State constabulary; and urging the withdrawal and removal of both these causes of irritation, in behalf of public peace and order.

The committee found Scott apparently ready to accede to any proposition that would insure quiet. He had just been reelected by an overwhelming majority, and, as far as he was concerned, there was no further need of all this political machinery. But it was necessary to try to conciliate the tax-payers of the State, whose sense of justice and fair dealing had been so grossly outraged by the means resorted to in the recent canvass. Whatever may have been the motives actuating him, he certainly did agree to both propositions, as promptly as his impediment of utterance would permit. He then and there authorized Capt. Estes to call in the State arms, and ship them to Columbia. He also promised the committee that his constabulary force would speedily be recalled – which promise he actually fulfilled a short time afterwards.

But Scott's conciliation could reach as low down as it ever aspired upwards; for, at the very time he was giving the committee a *private* audience, he had Joe Crews shut up in an adjoining chamber, with the door ajar, that he might hear every syllable uttered! The truth of this is founded on Joe's own statement, confirmed – for all his statements required confirmation – by the fact that Capt. Estes left him closeted with Scott when he returned to conduct the committee to the Governor's mansion. What use Joe made of this characteristic strategy will appear in the sequel. He certainly could testify to the time-honored adage, that eaves-droppers never hear any good of themselves.

These fruitful sources of annoyance and irritation being thus happily removed, the village and county of Laurens became as quiet and orderly as any other community in the State. The leaders were anxiously looking for some developments which they could magnify into "outrages," and thus keep up the notoriety they had already given the county, but they were never gratified. Attempts were thus made to distort some acts of sales-day rowdyism, but they always failed in these efforts at perversion, as it was easy to show that, in these, neither politics nor race was involved, but that they were the natural fruits of very mean whisky.

No efforts at investigating or arresting were made for months after the 20th of October, simply because there was no need for political capital of that sort just then. The previous course of the party, all over the State, had made it notorious that they cared nothing for these outrages and murders, in themselves considered, particularly when they were confined to the colored race; but when they could be made to subserve their party purposes, they could raise a howl which would reach from the Atlantic to the Pacific, and from the Lakes to the Gulf. How else can we account for the fact, now a part of history, that the high crimes of "conspiracy" and "murder," alleged to have been perpetrated, not only in Laurens, but in the counties of York, Union, Spartanburg, Chester, etc., in the fall of 1870, were ignored and unnoticed by the constituted authorities, till the spring of 1872. The policy is patent to the comprehension of a child. The elections were *over* in the fall of 1870, but another State election was to take place in 1872, and law and justice, to say nothing of the dignity of the State, must be kept in abeyance till then. Besides, a Presidential election was to be hotly contested the same fall, and this fortunate coincidence would add amazingly to the deep strategy of postponement. With such a capital of crimes and outrages whereby to "fire the Northern heart," there was no end to the aid and comfort they might expect from the authorities at Washington. The results of this policy more than realized their highest hopes, as we shall soon see.

About three months after the occurrence of the 20th October, there was a mere interlude in this matter of arresting, but from the character and circumstances of the parties selected for forcible seizure, public opinion at once assigned mercenary, and not political motives for the choice.

These parties were: Dr. D.A. Richardson, practicing physician, and Intendant of the town, Col. Jones, Sheriff of the county, Democrat; Col. Moseley, landlord of the only hotel in the place; Col. R.P. Todd, a prominent member of the bar; S.D. Garlington, apothecary and druggist; Capt. Hugh L. Farley, who, with Col. Todd and Mr. Garlington, represented some of the oldest and most respectable families in the county, and Mr. George Copeland, the wealthiest merchant in Clinton.

It was thought that these gentlemen, with the prospect of the penitentiary immediately before them, would "pay out" handsomely, either directly, or through their friends, should the opportunity be offered. It is always a risk to attribute motives, but in this case, public sentiment was, and still is, so unanimous in this charge *of black-mailing,* that nothing can change it.

These gentlemen were arrested by the State constabulary, and taken directly to Columbia, some time in January, 1871. The Richland Court was soon after in session, but the grand and petit juries had not yet been sufficiently manipulated for such trials as these. Those in charge of the prosecution, or rather, the legal representatives of the persecution, selected Dr. Richardson's case to go before the grand jury. What are commonly known as the Ku-Klux Acts of Congress had not then been passed, so he was indicted under the "Enforcement Act." The grand jury promptly threw this indictment overboard, by bringing in a verdict of "no bill." The Doctor thought he was free; but another warrant was ready for his arrest before he could leave the court-room. "No bills" were made out against the others, but they were excessively annoyed and harrassed for several weeks. They were many times haled from the jail to the court-house, to appear before the examining magistrate; every time amid the jeers, taunts and curses of a large crowd of colored spectators. As the magistrate would release one on insufficient evidence, Hubbard, the Chief Constable, with his congenial gang, stood ready to re-arrest him on some new warrant. This course was well calculated to extort blackmail, but it signally failed.

Worn out at length by this kind of persecution these prisoners determined to make one final effort, and, through their counsel, to apply for the writ of *habeas corpus.* This was still practicable, as martial law had not yet been proclaimed. Fortunately for them, Judge Vernon, a part of whose circuit was Laurens County, was within reach, and they decided to make their application to him. As this Judge had always proved upright and honest, and would, under no circumstances make his high office subservient to mere party purposes, he had himself become odious to the authorities, a stumbling block which must be moved out of their way, Accordingly, his impeachment was already determined upon, mainly, on the charge of intemperance, and a resolution to that effect was already before the Legislature, then in session.

Without hesitation, Judge Vernon determined to give the prisoners a hearing, through their counsel, and took his seat in the court-house, in Columbia, where the prosecution, as well as the counsel for the prisoners could be heard. In the midst of the proceedings, a dandified colored attaché of the Legislature walked in, and proceeding up to the bench, there deposited a written notification, that the "resolution of impeachment" had just been passed, and the day fixed for his trial.

The Judge merely glanced at the paper to learn its contents, and, without pause, proceeded with the cases. After a patient hearing, he admitted them all to bail in the sum of five thousand dollars each. Of course there was no loss of time in executing these bonds, nor was there any trouble about sureties, as the generous citizens of Columbia came forward in crowds, and voluntarily offered any number of the best names there.

And now it was amusing to witness the various exits of these gentlemen from Columbia. They knew that fresh warrants would await them at all the railroad stations, and that the constabulary would accompany all the outward bound trains. So each determined to find a route for himself, and on horseback, with the understanding that no two should travel the same road. Like a covey of partridges, suddenly flushed, they scattered to all the points of the compass, and after a few days, they reappeared in Laurens, dropping in one after the other, and from all possible directions.

But the strangest part of the story is, that though these heavy bonds were conditioned on their appearance at the Circuit Court of the United States, to be holden at Greenville Courthouse, on the following spring, not one of them was then summoned, nor were their bonds forfeited. And, though one or more of their number were re-arrested in the general onslaught on Laurens, in 1872, still not one of them has ever been brought to trial, while others subsequently arrested, *have* been tried. All this seems wholly unaccountable, excepting on the black mail theory.

The name of Judge T.O.P. Vernon, must not pass out of this narration, without some tribute to his noble self-sacrifice on this occasion.

There were few more promising young men than "Tom" Vernon, when he returned to his native county of Spartanburg, as a graduate from the University of Georgia, at Athens. Every celebration of the "Battle of Cowpens," every Fourth of July occasion, every public reception of distinguished visitors – in fine, every occasion calling for the orator or the ready speaker within reach – claimed his name as most prominent on the list. He had not been long at the bar, before the Legislature elected him "Commissioner in Equity," for his native district, which office he held for many years. Forced out against his will, as a candidate for Congress, he carried his own district almost unanimously, though unsuccessful in the congressional district.

He also served as Judge of the Inferior Court, established soon after the war, in the first or Johnsonian reconstruction.

After the second, and now existing reconstruction, he, unfortunately, permitted himself to be elected Judge of one of the Circuits, sheltering himself under the examples set by Orr and

Thomas, natives, who had already taken other Circuits. Very soon afterwards, his unswerving integrity checked many of the local schemes of the party, and he became obnoxious to cliques and rings. They soon determined to get rid of him, and on a charge of "intemperance," his impeachment was already determined upon. His habits were no worse than those of many of his associates on the Bench, and certainly no worse *since* his election than before. He knew enough of the party to be assured, that a little yielding on his part, and a few pledges for the future, would cause all these clouds to vanish into thin air. In the cases then before him, he knew, that remanding these Laurens prisoners to jail, would reinstate him with the party; and, on the other hand, his releasing them would be equivalent to signing his own deposition. He nobly decided on self-sacrifice in behalf of principle; and to disappoint their triumph and revenge, he resigned his commission before the day fixed for his trial.

CHAPTER SEVEN

☆　☆　☆　☆

Martial Law in Laurens

About the close of the year 1870, and the beginning of the next, the attention of the whole country was called to this naughty word – *Ku Klux* – by its appearance in an important State paper, no less dignified than the "Annual Message" of the President of these United States.

Upon this subject, it would be supposed, that the writer would be good authority, from what the reader will learn of his career in the sequel of this narrative. But he must confess, at the outset, that he has no personal knowledge of the mystic organization whatever – never having attended any of their meetings – never having witnessed any of their exhibitions – never having been associated with them in any way, or in any place, excepting in – the common jail.

That such secret conclaves did exist in certain counties in South Carolina, and that they were sometimes guilty of flagrant acts of lawlessness and outrage, cannot be denied; but the writer has good reason to know that these very acts were nowhere else more regretted than among all the respectable classes, in the very communities where they occurred.

There had been a time, in the history of this State, when the existence of such conclaves would have been a moral impossibility. The higher law of public opinion would have crushed them out at their very inception. But in these days, the times seemed sadly out of joint, and lawlessness and outrage became the order of the day, much more on the part of the oppressor than the oppressed; and to discountenance one set was only to encourage the other.

There is no doubt, that what afterwards became "the Ku-Klux," were, in their origin, simply organizations for self-defence – similar to those in Laurens, just before the outbreak on October 20th, 1870.

When all immediate danger of actual conflict was over, from the disarming of the militia and the withdrawal of the constabulary force, the more prudent and respectable withdrew from them, and they fell into the hands and under the control of those lawless and reckless spirits, to be found in almost every community – particularly after a protracted and disastrous war.

They have now run their career, and are heartily denounced by both friend and foe; but in the same category, may not something be said of the "Freedman's Bureau," the "Union League," and even those United States garrisons so often prostituted to the vilest and most reckless purposes? Take Major Merrill, in York County, as a notable instance, who degraded the uniform he wore, by such acts of cruelty and tyranny towards unprotected and helpless families, as the lowest Ku-Klux would have blushed to have acknowledged against the most obnoxious negro. The chief difference between them would be, that while the K. K. would try to justify himself, on the ground of self-defence, the gallant Major could only smirk at his superiors, and utter the overpowering argument, *"there is* MONEY *in it!"*

Bad as they were, the Ku-Klux became terribly magnified in their proportions, and their outrages were amazingly multiplied by those "wicked who flee when no man pursueth." Their fame had so spread abroad in the land, that they were not only specially noticed in the President's message, but became the subject of grave deliberation in Congress.

Early in 1871, the very strong legislation, known as the "Ku-Klux Acts," was already maturing at Washington, and rumors came thick and fast, that martial law was to be proclaimed in certain counties in South Carolina, including Laurens, of course.

Under this feeling of uneasiness and apprehension, a public meeting was called at the court-house, and a committee was appointed to go on to Washington. This committee was instructed to wait on the President, and make such representations of the true state of things, as to cause ours to be excepted from the list of the proscribed counties. Three of this committee, Hon. W. D. Simpson, chairman, R. S. Goodgion and J. A. Leland, promptly proceeded on their mission. But they soon found that the political machinery at the National Capital, was far too complex for them. There were rings and cliques, and "wheels within wheels," very available and exciting to the initiated, but exceedingly perplexing and disgusting to plain, blunt men. One of their number, Mr. Goodgion, armed with the truth and righteousness of his cause, even ventured to call upon B. F. Butler, at his lodgings, to appeal to his former States Rights principles, and his more recent professions as a vindicator of the rights of the oppressed. But he found the Massachusetts Representative as deaf as an adder to all such appeals, but showing so much of its venom, that he never repeated the call.

Through the kind attention of Senator Robertson, of their State, a private interview with the President was secured at an early date. Gen. Grant received them courteously and listened with commendable patience to the written statement read to him by Col. Simpson: but gave no evidence of the impression made upon his mind, one way or the other. His reticence may have been characteristic or politic, but it was most discouraging to the Committee, who had come so far for an interchange of information. They were prepared to give information or particulars which could not be embodied in a written document, and to be subjected to the closest cross-examination; but there was nothing of the kind. After the reading of the "statement," the President took possession of it and the accompanying documents, and simply saying that he would see to it that they should get before the Committee of Congress, at that very time engaged in considering the disturbances at the South, he politely bowed us out to make room for others.

These gentlemen left Washington with the profound impression that their visit had accomplished no good result. This impression became a conviction, when martial law was proclaimed; as Laurens was assigned a conspicuous place among the first of the counties thus distinguished.

By a proclamation of the President the "writ of *habeas corpus*" was suspended in seven of the counties of South Carolina early in 1872, and Laurens was about the first on the list.

Though long anticipated, when the crisis did come there was much of dismay and consternation. No one could feel safe when thus turned over to the tender mercies of these unscrupulous leaders. As there was no legal protection, no appeal to any tribunal, State or Federal, those who knew themselves to be obnoxious to Crews & Co., suddenly retired to parts unknown.

Judge J. L. Orr is reported to have said that he had thought the people of Laurens unjustly persecuted, until he heard of several of her prominent citizens running away from legal process, and, as he had never known an *innocent* man to run away from a threat, he was forced to change his mind, and lay aside all sympathy.

Col. Orr's opinion was worth very little with us, one way or the other, but even *he* would not have ventured that remark if he had lived at Laurens. No one was safe, whatever his position or previous character; and it had already been shown that prominent citizens could be hurried to jail, and that there was no limit to the number of false witnesses who were ready to swear to any statement put into their mouths, for money.

The sweeping arrests, afterwards made, showed that these men acted wisely; and if the whole white population could only have afforded a general exodus at that time, it would have prevented many weary months of heart-ache to some of her best families, and would have saved our great government one of its foulest blots.

It is a slander on these gentlemen, as well as on all the others arrested in Laurens County, to class them with the Ku-Klux. As before asserted in these pages, these organizations never gained a foothold in this county, through all the exciting events of reconstruction. The severe lesson taught our colored fellow-citizens on the 20th of October, 1870, had proved most salutary. They then found out, that however forbearing and long-suffering the white man had shown himself to be, there *was* a limit beyond which they could only go at the peril of their lives; pass that limit, and he would not only resist, but he would *kill*. Besides this argument, which the dullest brain among them could comprehend, they had been left alone, by these party-leaders, for nearly two years; and experience has shown, that, whenever this has been the case, there has been no trouble, nor bad blood between the races.

For a long time, therefore, the venerable town of Laurens had been as quiet and orderly as any New England village, in the time of the Puritans. Judge then of the surprise and consternation of her citizens at what happened to them on the 31st of March, 1872.

On that quiet Sabbath morning, just as the sun was rising, two formidable military bands, from opposite points of the compass, suddenly burst upon that devoted place. From the east, came a captain with a strong detachment of U.S. Infantry, who had marched all night from Newberry, some thirty-two miles distant. From the west, came a lieutenant with a body of U. S. Cavalry, who had also traveled all night from Union, some thirty-five miles off.

Soon every road leading from the village was securely guarded, and the work of arresting began most energetically. With two "Assistant United States Marshals," – Hubbard, accompanied by infantry, and Hendrix, accompanied by cavalry, – the whole town was soon ransacked from cellar to garret, and they made short work of it.

Now, why this sudden invasion of a peaceful community, with the same parade and dash as would have been expected if these people had been *then* engaged in acts of rebellion, or of flagrant insurrection? Can it be believed in this age and country, that all this was merely for *political effect?* And yet, this seems the only solution. Every thing was too civil and quiet in Laurens, in view of the State and Presidential elections, in the fall, and something had to be done to fire the colored heart, and to draw the party lines more sharply; and, besides, many of their schemes could much better be carried out, with some of these white leaders securely shut up in the four walls of a jail.

All the warrants of arrest were nearly identical. The charge was "conspiracy and murder," in that, on the 20th October, 1870 (some fifteen months previous), each one was a participant in the riot, on the day after the election; and had murdered several colored citizens, whose names were given. Soon the majority of the adult male population of the town, then present, were arrested; and, at first, shut up in the court-house. As soon as this congregation, without reference to sects, was assembled in this unusual place, and by such forcible means, we were marched, in procession, through Main street, to the residence of the Honorable Joseph Crews.

The marching through the streets, we could understand; it being, simply, an exhibition for the edification of the colored population. But why should we be domiciled in Joe's house? It would seem, either that he wished his sable constituents to see clearly that it was *his* work, or that he was ambitious of having some of the best citizens of the place under his roof, for once, at any rate, who never would have gone there voluntarily. In confirmation of this last surmise, it may, seriously, be remarked, that Joe, like the whole batch of carpet-baggers and scalawags, was exceedingly sensitive on this subject of social position. He found that, with all his ill-gotten wealth and political power, he was still looked upon as on the same level with the worst of his sable constituents, and his ambition, in this regard, even overcame his malignant revenge. For, it is a notorious fact, that he offered exemption from arrest to any who would sign a document certifying to his respectability and social position, up to the time of the war; and that there were found *men* who signed this paper – thus securing for themselves inglorious ease at home, but at the sacrifice of all self-respect.

But to return to our narrative. Thus huddled together in Joe's unfurnished parlor, we still constituted the greater part of the Presbyterian congregation, including two ruling-elders. We, therefore, invited the Rev. John G. Law to preach the afternoon sermon to us – which he did, most acceptably. John iii. 16.

About sunset, the order came to transfer us to the common jail; and we were again marched in procession down Main street, and the whole party – some twenty odd – were consigned to *dungeons.*

We found in the jail about an equal number of the citizens of Clinton, who had been brought up that morning by the United States infantry, on their march from Newberry.

The first night in jail was rather a gloomy one to most of the party; as the transition from comfortable homes to cells from which negro convicts had been but recently removed, was rather sudden and abrupt. A few, however, illustrated their faith by their resignation and contentment under the strange providence which had brought them there.

The writer's personal experience in these new and strange circumstances can be best learned from a journal, kept regularly during his imprisonment, and from which most of what follows in this narrative will be freely taken.

"March 31st, 1870. I rose early, dressed for church, and was reviewing my lesson for my Bible-class, when United States Marshal Hendrix rode up to the college, accompanied by two mounted men. On entering the room, he held out a warrant, endorsed 'United States *versus* J. A. Leland; *conspiracy and murder!*' Of course, I could only submit, but asked the privilege of eating breakfast before setting out on so novel a campaign. This was granted, and one of the soldiers was detailed to remain with me. After a hearty, but solitary breakfast, I merely bowed 'good-morning' to my household; and, pipe in mouth, sallied forth, followed by my guard, with his piece at a shoulder. Each window towards the gate was filled with the heads of the young ladies of the college – witnessing this strange exit of their president. * * * *

"April 1st. * * * * When ushered into the dungeons, last night, there were three or four of us to each cell, and no preparation for sleeping. The floors were very hard and very dirty, and no provision for ventilation. Our immediate predecessors having been negro convicts who had been confined for months, we had very sensible evidence of their influence on the atmosphere; and one of the party amused us with a serenade, emphasizing the lines:

'You may break, you may ruin the vase, if you will,
    But the scent of the roses will hang round it still'

"Our families and friends have sent us abundant supplies for breakfast, this morning, and, thus 'strengthened in the inner man,' we feel defiant. The Clinton roll, added to ours, swells our numbers to some forty, including two ruling elders, three physicians, and the others mainly merchants and farmers. * * * * *

"April 2d. * * * * Yesterday, friend T–– developed a new trait in his character, or rather, was transformed into a new man. Ordinarily, a very quiet, sober citizen; his friends regarded him as overmodest and retiring. But, on yesterday, he procured two or more bottles of spirits, of different kinds, and was very pressing for all to drink with him. He had the floor most of the afternoon, and was very violent, and even eloquent, in speech and gesture – using, sometimes, all four limbs – and all were amazed at the change that had come over him.

"This morning, I saw him sitting on a low box, with his elbows on his knees, and his head pressed between the palms of both hands – the picture of despair! In answer to my question, he had a long confession; the substance of which was, that this had been his first experience in tippling, and, by the help of God, it would be his last. That he had often seen those in trouble made, apparently, very happy by indulging in drink; and, he thought, if any one ever needed a solace of that kind, it was himself, on yesterday. But he had tried the experiment fully, and found that he had to pay for a few hours of delirium, by long hours of throbbing temples, and such mortification and self-reproach as overwhelmed him."

The writer selects the above extract for the benefit of temperance men. Friend T—— was as good as his word, and, from that day, has never been known to touch ardent spirits, even when prescribed by a physician.

"April 3d. We are under marching orders to-day. That detestable little Yankee Lieutenant of Cavalry, McDougal, had ordered us all to set out *on foot* for Union C.H., and only to take such baggage as we might be willing to strap to our backs. Our friends, however, have procured road wagons for our use, and, with difficulty, have obtained the consent of this petty tyrant for us to use them. We had been transferred from the cells to the common halls of the jail, after the first twenty-four hours, and have had free intercourse with our friends from the outside. Rev. Mr. Riley, pastor of the Presbyterian Church, visited us on yesterday, and presenting us with a Bible, requested us to promise that we would use it morning and evening, at 'family worship.' This promise was cheerfully and unanimously given."

And it was faithfully kept too. Whatever the surrounding circumstances might be, every morning and evening found us assembled for worship, with that Bible. No "family" has ever been more punctual, as there was no possibility of dodging. That Bible is now deposited in the Presbyterian Church in Laurens, on the table under the pulpit, as a memorial of the troublous past.

CHAPTER EIGHT

☆　☆　☆　☆

Journal of a Prisoner

As all the facts connected with our jail experience must be gathered from the journal already mentioned they may come fresher to the reader's notice, if quoted directly from its pages. The writer will, therefore, make free use of it in what is to follow.

"Union Jail, April 4th. Yesterday we had a most unpleasant wagon ride of thirty-five miles, through a cold, drizzling rain, to the common hall of this jail, which we reached long after night-fall. Our overcoats, etc., were completely saturated, and the jailor could furnish us with no dry blankets, as he said all of his had been burned up in efforts to stay the recent fire in this town. We had no lights, and only the fragments of our noon-day lunch. Yet we had our first 'family prayers;' the acting chaplain repeating the 23d Psalm from memory, with the Bible in his hands, and singing the hymn beginning, 'There is a fountain filled with blood.' Good Capt. Mc. afterwards declared, that while these exercises were going on, for the first time since his arrest, he 'felt a flood of light and comfort flowing into his soul.'"

With floors covered with several coats of tobacco juice, and with such moist bed-clothes as our bundles furnished, we did not enjoy our night's rest. Our kind friends in Union, Col. Young at their head, have provided for us a bountiful breakfast, spread

85

just in front of the jail, and which we can see through the bars; but as we are to take the train for Columbia, and it is nearly time for the whistle to blow, we begin to fear that our gallant little lieutenant intends to cheat us out of this creature-comfort too.

"Columbia, April 5th. The apprehension expressed in the record of yesterday was too well-founded; as we were kept under lock and key until the first whistle blew, and then hurried by the well-filled breakfast table without a chance to touch it. But we were only in a fitter plight to appreciate Mrs. Elkin's kindness at Alston. When we stopped there, all of us were crowded into her little reception room, where she soon presented herself with a two gallon coffee pot, quite full, and with the necessary trimmings.

"This Christian charity warmed our hearts as well as bodies, and we will not soon forget it. Here West gave the first symptoms of that pneumonia, from which he is now suffering so intensely. That cold wagon ride from Laurens was too much for his feeble frame.

"We reached this jail about sunset on yesterday, and were marched here from the depot some half a mile, 'two and two, Newgate fashion.' The procession was a gloomy one; thirty-six hungry and jaded men encumbered with all the baggage we had, and moving through the middle of the street with a mob of negroes of all ages and of both sexes, cursing and jeering at us from both side-walks. There was some delay at the door of the jail, until some negro convicts could be moved from the lower corridor of cells, to make room for us, when we were ushered into their places, and assigned six to a cell. Again supperless and without lights, we had our family worship, and, gloomily enough, passed our first night in Columbia.

"West becoming seriously ill, the jailor summoned the jail physician, who turned out to be Dr. Talley, whom had I known from his boyhood. From West's critical condition, he ordered him to be transferred to the second floor, where there were two adjoining rooms, with windows and fire-places, intended for officer's quarters. He also detailed me to nurse him with such assistants as I might deem necessary, and for whom I would become responsible. This was carried out this morning by placing West in the smaller of the two rooms, and in my calling for *eight* assistants, including all of our number who were fat and infirm. I would have called for more if accommodation could have been furnished them, as the doctor, in his kindness, had not restricted me in that respect.

"Our Presbyterian friends first found us out this morning, and as we had a case of 'sick, and in prison,' the ladies were about the first to 'minister to us,' and our back rations were soon abundantly made up.

"April 6th. From our experience on yesterday, I would most heartily recommend to any Ruling Elder who may be sent to jail, to select the institution in Columbia, particularly if he has a father's reputation to fall back upon. No Moderator of a Synod could have received more attention, nor could he have fared better than I did on yesterday. Not only the Elders 'who were in that city,' but the 'mothers in Israel,' and, outside of all church ties, representatives from almost every class of the old régime kept dropping in upon us. Thus our Laurens delegation soon found themselves transformed from Ku-Klux prisoners, ordered about by dirty little turn-keys, or dirtier little Lieutenants, into something like moral heroes or certainly into martyrs, in the eyes of those whose opinions we most valued, and the transition was a most grateful one." * * * *

Here follows the record of days and weeks of unwearied kindness and liberality on the part of our Columbia friends. During all our *four weeks* sojourn in their midst we never ate one morsel of jail rations, and our larder was kept constantly supplied with the best the market could afford. We knew that hams, turkeys, roast-pigs, fish, oysters, etc., were more frequently on our board than on the table of any hotel in Columbia, and our gratitude was in proportion. When it was ascertained that our stay was to be protracted, the ladies organized regularly for this work. Some would collect contributions, mainly from the merchants on Main street. Others would purchase and see to the preparation of the supplies, and a third party would see to their safe delivery at head-quarters. Mrs. John B. Adger was supervisor and treasurer, and at the close of our term in Columbia, she wanted the writer to accept, for distribution, in cash, the forty-five dollars surplus, then in her hands. This was declined, with many thanks, as we were then going to equally hospitable friends in Charleston. More than a year afterwards, when the writer had left Laurens, mainly on account of these very troubles, and was seeking a new home, with very limited means, Mrs. A. handed him this identical amount, as the representative of those for whom it was intended.

Mrs. Dr. Woodrow was the most constant of all our lady visitors. The Dr. would leave her at our door when he rode to deliver his lectures in the College, and call for her on his return home. Her bright face, sparkling wit, and cheery talks, became a necessity to us, and if ever she was prevented from dropping in, the day seemed lost. Her name has become a household word in all that section of country, from which the prisoners came, and in the heart-gratitude of those loving ones whom she may never see in the flesh; she already has her reward.

Mrs. Clara Leland, the step-mother of the writer, was as indefatigable as her other engagements would permit, and, had circumstances required it, would have shown the same self-sacrificing devotion to the son which she had already illustrated in the case of the afflicted father.

As to the sick man, West, the attentions of the ladies were unremitting. Mrs. Adger, particularly, became very much interested, and furnished his sickroom with new bedstead, bedding, bed-clothes, and many other conveniences. When his wife came down to see him, she sent her back with a large trunk of clothing for herself and her children. West, himself, soon began to convalesce under the tender nursing he received, backed by the constant attention of Dr. Talley. In three weeks he was strong enough to return home, and was presented by Mrs. A. with all the furniture of his sick chamber and the expenses of himself and family home. We will throw the mantle of charity over his subsequent career, which is an act of great forbearance on the part of a fellow-prisoner.

There were others of the good ladies of Columbia, as Mrs. Howe, Mrs. Peck, Mrs. Plumer, Mrs. McMaster, and others, whose alms and prayers we had constantly, but whose nerves shrunk from such a jail. Mrs. Howe and Mrs. Peck did venture once, however, and the effect on the latter I will not soon forget. She had been the life-long friend of my sainted mother, and her wild, distracted look is before me even now. "John Leland! *are you* in this horrid place?" Then glancing across the passage at the long row of assassin-looking negro convicts, and at the bars and bolts all around her, she choked down and said no more. I doubt whether an actual visit to the "Spirits in Prison" could have affected her more. But that *mother's* arm around my neck, and that warm mother's *kiss* meant more than all she could have said; and I went "in the strength thereof for forty days," at least. Other lady friends were frequently with us, but a simple record of their names must suffice just here. We kept a register in our "Bible," and now have the autographs of Mrs. C. D. Melton, Mrs. George Symers, Mrs. Preston Hix, Mrs. LeConte, Mrs. Goodwyn, Mrs. Taylor, Mrs. Boatwright, Mrs. Thornwell, Jr., Mrs. McCormick, Mrs. Horace Leland, Mrs. N. W. Edmunds, (the writer's only surviving sister; she and Mrs. Horace Leland did not reside in Columbia), Miss Percival, Miss Gussie Waltour, Miss Fickling, Miss May and Miss Smith.

Of the numerous sympathizers of the sterner sex, probably Dr. Plumer, and his son-in-law, Mr. S. S. Bryan, were the most constant. The latter was a Pennsylvanian, yet, though his powers of locomotion were very feeble, hardly a day would pass without his kind sympathy and pleasant words. Dr. Plumer brought two tin pails on his first visit, the one with a gallon of tea, ready sweetened, and the other of chicken soup. As there were more of our number complaining besides the sick man, these proved very acceptable. Every day after that, Sundays excepted, his rockaway would be seen at our gate; and balanced by the same tin-pails, with precisely the same quantity of tea and soup, his venerable form could be seen ascending our stairs. Where he obtained such a constant supply of chickens, in a market so variable as that of Columbia, was a puzzle to all of us but they never fell short in legs or wings. One day, there was an extra newspaper bundle under one arm, and on opening it before me, (I can hear his deep tones now), "We don't want you to give up too much, at *once!*" Saying this, he displayed a goodly pile of hanks of the finest Virginia smoking tobacco! A very sensible present it was, as it reminded me so often of the kind donor every day, and caused me to bless him so early every following day. Rev. Drs. Howe, J. Leighton Wilson, Jos. R. Wilson, Adger, Smyth, Girardeau, and Rev. Messrs. Green, Manning Brown, Wm. Martin and J.H. Thornwell, were frequently with us. From such a list, we had no difficulty in getting two sermons every Sunday, and very excellent lectures at our family prayers. The Theological Students also frequently came round, and conducted evening worship for us. Dr. Plumer distributed some of his own books, and Dr. Adger saw to it, that every one who needed it should be supplied with a neat copy of the New Testament and Psalms, bound together.

Eternity alone will develop all the fruits of these high religious privileges; but the writer knows of three cases, where they were most signally blessed. One of these was a gentleman of high standing, who, before his imprisonment, seldom attended church, and was rather skeptical in his views. A few weeks after his liberation, he appeared before the session of the Presbyterian Church in Laurens, on a profession of faith, and has since become a Ruling Elder and one of the pillars of the church. Whether such results as these did not compensate a thousand fold for all our troubles, is a home question, materially modifying the cry of "martyrdom."

Our "fellow-citizens," who honored us by their visits, constitute a very formidable list. Among them can be mentined, Col. Thomas, Dr. Miot, Dr. Smith, Gen. Preston, Col. McMaster, Col. Palmer, W.H. Trescott, R.L. Bryan, J.H. Kinard, and many others. Col. Thomas and Dr. Miot were the most constant and regular of these, and their matinee visits were always anticipated with much pleasure. The writer can safely assert, that at no previous visit to Columbia, and for the same length of time, had he ever seen so many of his friends, and so often.

General Preston's notions of *spiritual* comfort differed somewhat from the D.Ws. His remark to us was, "Well, gentlemen, we are all in jail in South Carolina; the only difference is, you are under shelter, and those of us who are on the outside, have to dodge the storm as best we can." Soon after he left, he sent us a five gallon keg of *lager beer.* For want of something better, we drew it off in water buckets, and thus distributed it up and down stairs. Never has lager beer been served in more generous bumpers, and never was a keg more expeditiously despatched. And as to the quantities imbibed, some found they had deceived themselves, while trying to deceive their neighbors.

Neither were all efforts at entertainment on one side. Capt. McCarley, the oldest of our number, was the greatest ladies' man we had. Ben Ballou, with his whistling, accompanied by the guitar, would outdo the mock-bird itself at its own notes. And the irrepressible Sim. Pearson was the life of the whole party in practical jokes, and a cheerfulness that nothing could interrupt. He had spent some months in a Northern prison during the war, and his jail experience was invaluable to us. A very energetic, industrious farmer at home, he made the most of the small area he now had, for physical efforts. He was sweeping the floor constantly, while daylight lasted, and if any stray newspaper fell in his way, it was sure to go into the fire. He said he had not read one of them since the war, and he never intended to read one again. Once he was seen with his head bowed almost between his knees, as he sat on the edge of his bunk. Some one, rallying him on having the "blues," he said: "I was just thinking that my poor wife had been bothering me, all spring, to let her have the horses for just three hours to go and see her mother, and I always answered her that I could not possibly spare them. Now, just to think, she has had them for three weeks, to go just where she pleases!" Then with one or more perpendicular leaps, followed by successive somersaults, without regard to the impenetrability of his neighbors, he would scatter his cares to the winds. The only memorial he kept of his farm, was a small onion-set, planted in a *match-box* filled with earth, and kept constantly on the mantel-piece. Mrs. Woodrow fell heir to this, at last, and took it with her on her three years' sojourn in Europe. Now that she has returned home, she has the same box with the same earth in it, and waiting for Sim. to renew his crop.

When Mayor McKenzie presented us with a box of assorted candy, Sim. became confectioner with some mercantile devices not known to the outer world.

CHAPTER NINE

☆　☆　☆　☆

Journal Continued

To resume the Journal, so long suspended:

"April 8th. After having been allowed more than a week to become acquainted with our new quarters, we were summoned to-day, for the first time, before the United States Commissioner. It looks somewhat strangely, to be arrested under a warrant, requiring our immediate presence before the Commissioner, and then to be left in jail for ten days, before any call is made. But we must remember, this is *Reconstruction*.

"We were marched in procession with one assistant U. S. Marshal at the head, and another in the rear, nearly the whole length of Main street, down to the State House. Of course this exhibition was much enjoyed by the 'lewd fellows of the baser sort,' black and white, who so constantly infest the streets of Columbia. The room occupied by the Commissioner was well supplied with chairs, but these were all filled by greasy wenches, who sat there to enjoy the spectacle of white men brought to grief. The Commissioner himself (Boozer) is a poor creature, a mere tool of Joe Crews, without whose instructions he says nothing in these cases. Joe was sitting by his side and looking more like a culprit than any of those before him. We were asked when we would be ready for a hearing before the Commissioner? As spokesman for the party I answered, 'just *now,* and just *here,* as we are anxious to learn what has brought us from our homes at this busy season, to the jail in Columbia.' After a whisper from Joe, Boozer replied, 'but the government is not ready, and can't be for a week or more.' With this encouraging information we were marched back in the same order, having contributed something to the fees of these officials, Marshals and Commissioner. No other motive could be seen for the parade."

Before making the next extract, it may be well to premise what was exactly the participation of the writer in the riot of 1870, for which his warrant stated he had been arrested.

As already mentioned in this narrative, the exercises of the Female College had been resumed on that day, at nine o'clock, A. M., the writer was there at his post. He continued teaching his classes till two P.M., the usual hour of closing, perfectly unconscious of what was going on on the public square. The college is a quarter of a mile distant from the scene of action, and the wind was blowing so violently towards the square that he did not even hear the guns. At two o'clock parents sent to request him to retain their daughters at the college, as there was much excitement "down street."

On learning the true state of the case and that perfect quiet had been restored, he formed into a squad the young ladies living beyond the square, and marched at their head past the scene of disturbance. This was the only bellicose act on his part during that eventful day, and the young ladies are ready to testify that no negro – man, woman or child – was seen by them on their whole line of march. As the riot had taken place at 11 A.M., in all probability there was not another citizen of Laurens who knew less of it than the writer, until he was informed of it some three hours after it was all over.

Now for the

Farce in the Court House.

"April 18th. At four o'clock this afternoon we were all marched to the court-house, and there we found Boozer sitting in the Clerk's chair, with Joe Crews by his side, and the house packed with colored spectators of both sexes. Col. W. D. Simpson and Mr. Jaeger had kindly offered their professional services as counsel, and we were soon all seated within the bar. Boozer made short work of the Clinton prisoners. A single witness, very black, and with a very loud voice, one of whose names was 'Ferguson,' testified against the whole batch, and on his single oath, all eighteen were remanded to jail for trial. Seldom, even in these ridiculous pretensions to the forms of law, had there been a more outrageous case of false swearing than in this man Ferguson. To have seen all, he swore to having seen, in one dark night, and at points miles apart, he must have exceeded the owl in night vision, and a Salem witch in powers of locomotion.

"The Laurens C. H. prisoners were taken up separately, and some estimate of the testimony against each can be formed from what was sworn to in my case. The first witness was a boy named George Allen, (or 'Mr. *All-in,*' as the prosecuting attorney, Dunbar, called him). He swore that Major Leland was on the ground from breakfast time till dinner, and that he was shooting and 'cussin and swearin' all the morning. That he himself saw him shoot several times, and heard him 'cuss.' Col. Simpson made him repeat some of the oaths distinctly, so that the Commissioner might take them down in writing, and they were so ridiculous and original that I could not refrain from laughing, and the little rascal joined me in the laugh more than once.

"The second witness, 'Lame Peter,' said nothing about the oaths, but made me shoot almost as often as 'Mr. All-in' did.

"The third witness, 'Young,' (for there were three of them) was much more moderate as to the number of shots, but made me shoot in a very novel way. He said he saw me stand at the public well and shoot down an alley, near the armory, where William (somebody) was killed. Now to do this, my bullet must have gone along one side of a triangle, and then turn, sharply, at an angle not very obtuse. Col. Simpson calling the attention of the 'Court' to this fact, Lahew, or Lehay, or some such name, belonging to the 'constabulary,' was called, and *he* made oath that it could easily be done!

"Here the 'government' closed, and Mr. Jaeger was about to make a speech in my behalf, when I begged him to desist. That such evidence would disgrace a sombre Court in Dahomey, and was unworthy of serious notice. That the 'Court' had already announced that he was bound to believe every statement, under oath, however absurd or impossible, and not to admit any evidence whatever on the part of the prisoner. Under such circumstances, that it would be a waste of breath and time to make any argument. As we were talking on this point, the Commissioner announced that, as it was late, he would suspend the matter just then, and resume tomorrow, at ten o'clock.

"While the last witness was speaking, a storm of wind struck the court-house, of sufficient violence to throw down a half-finished building on Market street. It seemed as though the very elements strove to drown the voice of the perjurer.

"We were marched back to jail through a driving rain, and went immediately to our evening worship. We alluded to the false witnesses who had risen up against us, in humble imitation of Him who once prayed: 'Father, forgive them; they know not what they do.'

"April 19th. A messenger came in this morning to announce that Boozer had been taken suddenly sick, and that there would be no court to-day. I understand, perfectly, the object in these delays. Joe is more anxious for *money* than revenge; and he is hoping at every stage in these proceedings, to have a goodly pile of greenbacks offered by my friends for my release. But he will find that 'hope deferred maketh the heart sick,' if he has *any* heart.

"Soon after the exciting events, above recorded, the writer was forcibly reminded how precarious a thing human reputation is, and how the truth of history may be distorted.

"Sam. B. was regarded among us as a 'good fellow,' but he had a very had habit of profane swearing. Something had happened which greatly excited him, and he was pouring out a perfect cascade of his choicest oaths. Stepping up behind him, and tapping him on the shoulder, I reminded him of our promise 'to run this machine,' without cursing or whiskey. At once, changing his tone, he replied, with his peculiar smile, 'Well, Major, you can say anything to me, and I am always glad to listen. But in this thing of *profane swearing,* you ought to be a little cautious. What you know of my swearing is only *hearsay,* but, in your case, it is *a matter of record!'*

"April 20th. Again we were paraded before the commissioner, and both Col. Simpson and Mr. Jaeger made earnest speeches in my behalf. But they soon after found out what kind of a head they were trying to impress. He actually announced that his office compelled him to believe all evidence given under oath, even if it involved physical and moral impossibilities. Under such a ruling, of course, our counsel declined to take any further part in the proceedings, and from that time on, there was such swearing against the rest of our number, as must have made the angels weep.

"At the close of this judicial farce, the prosecuting attorney (Dunbar) moved that Major Leland be bailed out till the November term of court, and the others be remanded for trial at the present term. But – on a whisper from Joe – the commissioner decided to remand all of us." So the word now is, "On to Charleston," where the United States Circuit Court is now sitting.

"April 22d. Yesterday (Sunday) was a day of very unusual privilege to me. Without my knowledge, my good friend, Capt. McCarley, had got the deputy jailor to promise, not only to let me attend the Presbyterian Church, but to go with me himself, instead of sending a United States soldier as my guard. It was the last day of the session of Presbytery, and, as usual, the 'Communion Sunday.' I had the pleasure of hearing an excellent sermon from my cousin, Rev. Charles Vedder, D. D., (Psalm xcii. 12), and when the communicants were invited forward, I hastened to reach the very seat my sainted mother had occupied, on such occasions, for more than a generation. But when I saw her life-long friends – Mrs. Peck, Mrs. McFie, and Mrs. Howe – come forward, and

take the seats nearest me, on the right, on the left, and immediately opposite, my heart swelled; and, for the first time since my
arrest, my eyes began to overflow. I learned more of what is
meant by 'the communion of saints,' at that table, than I had ever
known before, and my tears were not such as we hastily brush
away. I never expect to experience such feelings again, unless
when summoned to sit close by that sainted mother at the 'Mar-
riage Supper of the Lamb.'"

"It was a novel sight to see a ruling elder, at the church
served, for so many years, by his venerated father, sitting at the
communion-table under the guard of a deputy jailor, and to be
taken back to a murderer's cell, as soon as he should be dis-
missed! But his brethren seemed to view the matter in their own
way, by their manner of crowding around him, as soon as the
services were over. The Deputy himself was much impressed,
and called out, 'Do, Maj. L., go and take dinner with any one of
your friends, and come back to the jail when it it suits you!' But
I told him 'it was not so denominated in the bond,' and I would
go straight back with him. On our walk back to the jail, he expressed himself as much pleased with all he had seen and heard.
I then remarked that as he had gone to the morning service, on
my account, I would be glad to go to the evening service on *his.*
To this he readily assented, and called for me last night, accompanied by his wife; and we heard an excellent sermon from Rev.
Dr. Joseph R. Wilson.

"Yesterday was the second time I had passed the gate
since the rainy afternoon of our arrival; and I was surprised to see
the trees all clothed in green. When I last saw them, they were
under bare poles, stript for the storms of March.

"April 23d. As I found myself in a straight and narrow
lane, leading directly to the Albany Penitentiary, I began to look
around for some human aid, as the command is to *watch* as well
as pray. Under this 'suspension of the *habeas corpus,*' there was
no tribunal, State or Federal, to which I could appeal. I then remembered my old friend Stephen J. Field, once my classmate at
Williams College, Mass., now Associate Justice of the Supreme

Court of the United States, from California. I had renewed my acquaintance with him, most pleasantly, in my recent visit to Washington; when, as one of a committee, I had gone there to intercede with the President, to prevent these very judicial outrages that have now come upon us. Judge Field had invited Col. Simpson and myself to dine with him, on that occasion, and, on parting at the close of a very pleasant evening, he had made me promise to call on him, if ever I thought he could serve me.

"On yesterday, I thought the time had come, and I wrote him a long Iliad of woes, beginning with my arrest, and ending with the scene in the court-house. I told him, that, just at this time, the road to the Penitentiary was very short and direct, in this latitude. That under the direction of any prominent radical or scalawag, the magistrate was *bound* to issue his warrant; then, the United States Commissioner was *bound* to remand for trial; then, the packed grand jury was *bound to* find a 'True Bill;' then, the equally packed petit jury was *bound* to find a verdict of 'guilty;' and the judge was not only *bound* to send to the Albany Penetintiary, but was the very old *Bond* himself! That I had already taken two of these five steps, and I would look to him to block the lane in some way, or have me thrown over the fence."
* * * *

(This letter secured the release of *all of us* a very short time afterwards.)

"April 24th. Some ten days ago, Hubbard, the Marshal, selected one of the Clinton prisoners, Mark — by name, and placed him in solitary confinement, among the negro convicts, restricting his rations to bread and water. This Mark was an ignorant, weak foreigner, who had located at Clinton but a short time before his arrest. Every day, Hubbard would take him to the Commissioner's office, and, in a few hours afterwards, would bring him back to his cell. As all communication was cut off on our side, we could only conjecture the object of all this. Yesterday, however, he was released, and confessed that he had been starved into swearing some statement against his Clinton friends, but will not divulge what it is.

"We conjectured, all along, that this was the object, as many 'swift witnesses' had been manufactured in the same way, in the cases from York County. Select the proper subject, terrify him with threats, and reduce him to the very verge of starvation; *then* offer him his liberty and a small pecuniary reward, and such creatures as Mark are ready to swear to anything prescribed. *Now,* the rumor is, that the Clinton prisoners are to be taken to Charleston, *at once.*

"April 25th. And they were taken down that very afternoon. About 4 o'clock P. M., the word came for all them to get ready for the night train at 7 P. M., and soon afterwards we heard the rattling of *hand-cuffs,* thrown out in the passage below. Dr. Craig and Sim. Pearson, of my mess, at first thought that only a few would be subjected to that indignity, but both of them were soon summoned down to join the procession. Sim. called for an artist, to have the scene photographed, and, failing in this, he insisted that a chain should be put around his neck, and the other end given to that *very* black witness, Ferguson, mounted on a *very* white mule. He thought this would cap the climax to all the Ku-Klux shows yet exhibited in Columbia, and he was willing to take the leading part.

"Unfortunately, just at this time, Dr. Plumer, Mrs. Woodrow, and Miss Gussie W. entered the passage, and witnessed the process of hand-cuffing these eighteen gentlemen. Mrs. W., who had heretofore enlivened us with her wit and exhaustless humor, came running up to my room, nearly convulsed, her sobs almost tearing her little frame to shivers. In vain did I threaten to *switch* her, for proving such a cry-baby at last; for a time she was past all rallying. Miss Gussie took her stand at the window, in my room, to see the procession pass out of the gate. As the leaders first appeared, she swayed herself backwards, till, I thought, her spine must crack, and bringing both clenched fists down on the window-sill with all her force, and, as though there were no bones in them, she hissed out, 'Oh, that I could smite you all to the *centre* of the earth!' Then turning to us, her eyes actually sparkling light, she exclaimed, 'Mrs. Woodrow, *is* there a God in heaven, who can look on this, and not *smite* these wretches – not open the earth beneath their feet and swallow them all? I *am* bad, I feel *very* bad now, and I fear this sight will make me an infidel!' Old Capt. McCarley, sitting next to me, whispered, 'Major, that girl is an *angel!*' Mrs. W., overhearing this, rallied enough to whisper behind her hand, *'Fallen* angel!'

"Even a scene like this did not disturb Dr. Plumer's equanimity, and, even here, he could utter exactly the right words, at the right time. Glancing through the window at the procession, and coming to my side, he said, solemnly, 'Major Leland, remember, that all the time our Saviour was upon earth, he was *a citizen of a subjugated country!'* * * * * Our Clinton friends behaved like men, and we were not ashamed of them in any particular.

"April 26th. I have, once or twice, mentioned 'negro convicts' in this Journal, as faring very roughly. But there is a notable exception, in the person of a dandified imported negro, from Beaufort, I think, who has been sentenced to so many months *imprisonment,* for stuffing ballot-boxes, making false returns, etc. His apartments are near ours, and furnished in a style to do credit to a first-class hotel. He has there several of the 'members chairs,' and two of the veritable '$5 spittoons,' from the State House. He sometimes takes his meals in his quarters, but, generally, he is out on the streets from *early* in the morning till *late* at night. Says he is reading law with one of the sable practitioners – Elliott, perhaps. Take either one of our friends, in his cell down stairs, and this fellow in his room upstairs, and we have a very good illustration of the state of things *outside* too, particularly as the white man is only under a *'charge,'* and 'malicious,' at that, and the negro is already *tried and convicted!*

"April 27th. Our roll is dwindling very fast. Since the Clinton men left, in a body, our village prisoners have become much reduced in force. Called before the Commissioner *very* often – fees, $2 each for each hearing – they have successively been allowed bail till the November term, until our number is reduced to *four.* These are Capt. McCarley, Dr. McCoy, Dr. Black, and myself. Even with this small number, we are still separated, Drs. McCoy and Black being still confined to the corridors down stairs. Beverly Potter was the last to leave us to-day. I miss him very much. I regard him as true a man as ever went to a Ku-Klux jail, or kept out of it, either. His goodness of heart is unfailing. When that poor creature, West, was so ill, and the ladies could not be with him at night, Potter sat by his bed-side three nights in succession, watching over him, and nursing him as faithfully as ever mother watched and nursed her offspring. In the mess, he was always making sacrifices for the benefit of others, even in the culinary department. He was rather prolix in telling a story, but I wish he was here to-night to tell me another."

CHAPTER TEN

☆　☆　☆　☆

Journal Concluded

"April 28th. We heard from the Clinton delegation to-day, and they informed us that they had rather a rough time of it going down. After they had been paraded through the streets of Columbia, in handcuffs, they were locked up in the same car, with the colored witnesses against them, including the famous 'Ferguson.' Arrived in Charleston, they were marched a mile and a half through the streets to the 'House of Correction,' formerly known as the 'Sugar-House.' But kind friends were awaiting their arrival, and they were faring now even more sumptuously than they had done in Columbia.

"Under the inspiration of this letter, I immediately sat down, and penned the following doggerel lines, addressed to Sim. Pearson. Its insertion here is only excusable on the same ground that Dr. Johnson professed himself pleased with the dancing-dog – 'not that the dog danced so well, but that the dog could dance *at all':*

> My dear friend Simeon,
> I have the opinion,
> *Your* motto is now grown bigger;
> "Whatever is, is right!"
> "Let it come day or night,
> From heaven, earth or hell, man or nigger."

When I saw you hand-cuff'd,
I thought *now* he is bluff'd,
No chance, now, to show the "Old Rebel;"
But, as if led out to dance,
You seemed seeking this chance
To spite both Joe Crews and the debble.

In this right down hard luck,
I admired your pluck,
And will publish it home and abroad;
Let man do his worst,
Though with rage he may burst,
"Old Sim" mocks them, with strength fresh from God.

I have missed you, my friend,
In my snug little den;
Though friends have been kinder than ever;
I miss all your capers
Your burning my papers,
Your cooking and sweeping, so clever,

Friend Craig, too, I need
My newspapers to read,
He's gone, I can't make an impression,
I'm afraid he'll grow bold,
With no Captain to scold,
Each sin, and each little transgression.

Now, the Captain and I
Can go under the sky,
And sit in the sun, when he shines
Though we know 'tis still jail,
And we cannot give bail,
None hear from us murmurs or whines.

Still our lady-friends come,
Each fresh from her home,
To cheer us in this long confinement;
We love their sweet smiles,
We admire their wiles,
To cheat us all back to refinement.

We had ice-cream to-day,
A large churn, without pay,
Sent by these same ladies, God bless them
Each ate his own dish up,
And even friend Bishop
Was so full that he wished to caress them.

West went off to day,
Quite bright and so gay;
With a trunk from these same ladies' bounty;
Rich gifts and some pelf
For his wife, chicks and self;
(He's made money by serving his country).

Now, Simeon, my friend,
Where *will* this all end?
"That's not on us *now!*"
You say with a bow;
Well, I believe you are right,
So, "old fell," good night!
Don't kick up a row,
Nor get "under cow."

"April 30th. The Captain and I have had to apologise to our friends, both ladies and gentlemen, for trespassing on their kindness and hospitality so long, quoting the language of Charles II. on his death-bed, that he was an unconscionable long time in dying, and he hoped his friends would excuse him, as he would never do so again. Their reply was that they had had their jail visits as a part of the programme for each day, for so many weeks, that they would feel at a loss when we left, and would miss the excitement and the stimulus to patriotism and good works.

"The Captain and I, 'true yoke fellows,' are the only occupants of our large room. From the morning of our arrest to this pleasant afternoon we have never been out of the reach of each other's voices, excepting when I went to Church, through his kindness. I can safely say that in all these days, nights and *weeks,* no unpleasant word, act, or look has ever passed between us. Neither one of us is remarkably good-natured at home, but our temperaments seem to be exactly fitted to one another in jail.

"It is astonishing how human nature can accommodate itself to any change of circumstances, however violent the transition may at first appear. Here I have been *in jail* for one whole month, on a charge of "conspiracy and murder" and am constrained to look back upon this time as one of the most pleasant visits I have ever paid to Columbia. Physically, I have been very comfortable. Could rise as early in the morning as I pleased, and, from the abundance of hydrant water, could indulge my amphibious propensity for bathing, to the top of my bent. From the generous supplies of loving hearts, I could have my meals at any hour to suit my purposes, and our old family servant, Polly, a distinguished laundress, kept my 'chest' well supplied. Socially, morally *and* intellectually, the list of names, already given in these pages, the books and papers they so constantly furnished us, and the sweet and frequent correspondence with loved ones at home, and with old College friends and former pupils, both in and out of the State, all show that there was little danger of time hanging heavily on our hands.

"And then our religious privileges, not only in listening to some of the best sermons we have ever heard, but in holding sweet converse with these eminently gifted and godly men.

"With all these resources within, how contemptuously could we look down upon the pigmy tribe of Radicals and scalawags, who were trying to convince themselves that they were persecuting and degrading us. Joe Crews, sometimes comes sneaking along the passages, but any stranger would take him for the culprit, nor would he miss it, either.

"I forgot to record, in the proper place, that we were assured in a mysterious way, when we first arrived, that by paying $250 each, we could all be released. In response, we passed a unanimous resolution, that we would not pay one cent more than the law might force out of us.

"Charleston, May 1st. I was interrupted, in my moralizing

in Columbia jail, yesterday afternoon, by the entrance of Mrs. Woodrow, Mrs. Clara Leland and Mrs. Hix, who informed us that we were to be taken to Charleston, on the night train, and that they had come to see us off. Mrs. W. had brought wreaths for our wrists, should we be handcuffed, and they were talking quite bravely of what they had prepared to say to the officials, when the time came. I told them we had no doubt they felt so then, but when the time *did* come, they would find themselves much more demoralized than when spiders and bugs fell on them. I had almost to force them to their carriage, when the time approached, and it was none too soon. Mrs. W. presented the Captain and myself each with a rosebud,[1] to be worn in our buttonholes, charging us to keep them as long as she would the 'match-box,' which she then and there appropriated.

"Immediately after they left us, there was a clanking of steel in the passage below; and on being summoned down, we saw the tableau of Drs. McCoy and Black, bound together by 'hooks of steel,' and standing as immovable as statues. Soon one of these bracelets was adjusted to my left wrist, but when they attempted the Captain, it could not meet. A second and a third pair were tried, with like results. A fourth experiment caused the clasping, but only by tight squeezing. The fact is, the Captain had the wrist of 'a son of Anack,' and that saved us. I pledged myself to the Marshal, that I would hold his hand in mine, all the way to the depot, if he would only release him from the danger of strangulation, and this seemed to touch whatever there was of humanity in him, for he immediately released us all, saying, 'If I can't handcuff one, I won't handcuff any.'

"On our march to the depot, we recognized the carriage of our friends, near a corner where we had to pass. As we came to the nearest point, Capt. Mc. waved *both* hands, in token of the absence of handcuffs, and three white handkerchiefs, enthusiastically tossed from the windows of the carriage, was the last we saw of these loving hearts, in our jail campaign.

---

1. Both of us have our rosebuds still – 1878.

"We, too, were locked up with our colored witnesses, in the same car; the design, evidently, being to give them an opportunity to triumph over, and insult us, if they pleased. In this, however, they were disappointed. These poor creatures believed that they were engaged in a money speculation. They were receiving a handsome per diem, and what seemed to them, large sums for repeating, under oath, what had been put into their mouths; and this, they thought, was the easiest way of earning money they had ever tried. They felt no animosity against the prisoners. In fact, they tried to entertain us with their songs and stories, and, at the different stations, were always ready to wait on us, in purchasing supplies, whenever called on.

"Arrived in Charleston, we, too, were marched through the streets, and conducted to the common jail. Here, as in every other change of base, our experience was rather rough, at *first*. The jailor, receiving us as 'Ku-Klux prisoners from the up-country,' had us conducted to his most secure stronghold. This was the third story of his 'tower,' a cylindrical structure, with cells, on each story, opening on a narrow circular passage – like the holes in a circular mouse-trap. In this passage I am now pencilling these lines, in no very enviable frame of mind.

"May 2d. The United States jailor at the 'Sugar house' claimed us as *his* guests, on yesterday afternoon, and, as our board had cost him very little, so far, was glad to transfer us to these more liberal quarters. Here we are again with our Clinton friends, a large hall being assigned for our exclusive use. Our friends were enthusiastic on the subject of Charleston hospitality. Abundant meals were furnished, twice a day, in large hamper baskets, and facilities afforded for spreading a regular table. At night, a lady surprised me with a basket of *sea-crabs,* sent ready-boiled; and I had to dissect and eat more than a half dozen, before I could satisfy the curiosity of my up-country friends. When I would take off the back of a she-crab, unusually fat, some one would cry out, 'Oh, Major, throw that one away; *it's rotten!'* They called my breaking into the house of a live oyster, 'eating them *with the bark on.'*

"Hams and turkeys always did taste better to me, in that latitude, than elsewhere; particularly when flanked with rice, rightly boiled – potatoes, where the 'bark' scarcely adhered, and such vegetables as can only be found in Charleston market. I am not much of an epicure, but my jail experience has given a wonderful zest to such creature-comforts.

"W. D. Porter, Dr. Whitefoord Smith, Rev. Charles Vedder, Rev. W. B. Yates, George H. Walter, Capt. F. W. Dawson, John E. Carew, Dr. Parker, and W. Aiken Kelly, with others, spent the evening with us, and it turned out a very pleasant reception.

"Dr. Smith handed me a letter from Rev. Thos. G. Herbert, an old friend, and 'Presiding Elder of the Spartanburg District.' I knew this good brother was living on 'short commons,' with his limited salary, and large family; and when I found a $5 note enclosed, I was affected with a very choking sensation. I had received many highly prized letters, filled with noble Christian sentiments and sympathy; but it was left for this good Methodist brother to superadd *all his living* – for that day, at least.

"It is not as fashionable here for ladies to visit the jail, as it was in Columbia, but a very pleasant company did come round this morning, attracted by the sight of a ruling elder among jailbirds. Mrs. M. A. Snowden, Mrs. Hibben Leland, and Mrs. Chapin, did form a very pleasant family-group, and made me feel at home again.

"But I ought to feel very uneasy, as the morning papers announce that the grand jury have found 'true bills' against the whole batch of us, for *'Conspiracy and Murder'!* They probably took up our cases in the gross, without looking at the names at all, as they reported one name, the owner of which is now quietly at home, never having been even arrested. The docket is all clear, and our cases come next. Hon. W. D. Porter,[2] our lawyer, has been indefatigable in our behalf; and, as he seems confident, I am

2. Mr. Porter had no bill against me for professional services; but he has the life-long gratitude of many loving hearts.

determined 'not to cross the bridge, before I come to it.'

"May 3d. Our Laurens C. H. delegation, of four, have only been in Charleston two days and two nights, when it was announced to us, this morning, that Judge Bond had decided to adjourn the court, and admit us all to bail in the sum of $5000 each!

"Sweet has been the sympathy of friends, during these weary weeks of helplessness, and their unwearied kindness and attentions have deeply impressed our hearts; but now the cry is *Liberty* and *Home.*

"Loud are the encomiums and thanks heaped upon my highly respected friend of happier days, the Hon. W. D. Porter; but, without saying any thing about it, *I* 'see the hand of Joab' in all this, and my heart is welling with gratitude to the earlier friend of my halcyon days, my old classmate in Williams College, then called 'Steve Field,' but now, 'the Hon. Stephen J. Field, Associate Justice of the Supreme Court of the United States.'

"But from the lowest depths of a heart, now almost dissolving in gratitude, come overwhelming thanksgiving and praise to that God 'who ruleth in the affairs of men,' and 'who turneth the hearts of men even as the rivers of water are turned.'

"We were soon in procession for the court-house, to execute our bonds. There were some ladies with us, even at this early hour, and Mrs. Chapin was noticed to snap some implement in her pocket, which sounded like the loud clicking of the pistol-lock. Being asked what it meant, she replied, 'just let one of those darkies on the opposite side of the street dare to hoot at these gentlemen, and I will show you what I will do!' They did *not* hoot however, and we had a quick and joyous march.

"My good cousin Vedder had already prepared my bond, with Messrs. Robert Adger and J. A. Enslow as sureties, and I had only to step to the clerk's desk and sign, when I was once more *free.* But I stuck to my comrades till the last bond was signed; neither did it require much time, as the court-room was soon filled with willing securities.

"I am now busy packing up for home, and jot down these last lines, in this strange, eventful story. I must call on friend Vedder, and 'Miss Ammie,' now under the same roof, and on George H. Walter, on my way to the railroad, and then ——!

"Now, that it is over, I greatly prize this chapter in my history; for I have learned much I never knew before. Without affectation or cant, I have seen and tasted the goodness and loving-kindness of a covenant God, always faithful to all His promises. I have experienced the transforming influence of His presence on all things and every scene, however dark and mysterious. From the beginning, and all through this strange episode in my life, I have felt a large share of that confidence which inspired David to write that precious Psalm, 'The Lord is my Shepherd, I shall not want.' My body has been in the power of my persecutors, but the ME at which they seemed to aim was as far beyond their reach, and as safe, as the highest archangel in heaven; for I felt that I was protected by the same power, and comforted with the same love. The following lines express, very beautifully, my feelings, on closing this part of my Journal:

"Thy Presence has a wondrous power,
The sharpest thorn becomes a flower,
   And yields a rich perfume.
Whate'er looked dark and sad before,
With happy light shines silvered o'er,
   There's no such thing as gloom!

Thou knowest I have a cross to bear,
The needed stroke Thou wilt not spare,
   To keep me near Thy side;
But when I see the chastening rod,
In Thy pierced hand my Lord, my God,
   I feel so satisfied."

Over the joyous return home, the curtain must now drop, and the reader left to his own imagination. It will be noticed, that very little is said about home and its loved ones, in the foregoing pages. This has not been owing to any lack of materials, as a much larger collection could have been made from that source. But these are among the sanctities of life, "wherewith the stranger intermeddleth not."

In this connection, a single allusion to a now sainted daughter – my daughter Rebecca – may be pardoned. She left us, not long afterwards, and her early death was, no doubt, hastened by the shock of my arrest, and the long weeks of anxiety and apprehension which followed. Her correspondence, during this trying time, is treasured as the choicest legacy she could have left us. The writer learned to reverence his own child, who taught him much of that "wisdom that cometh down from on high." Her rapid ripening for heaven was the theme of all who were brought in contact with her; and the writer can now thank God that she has been removed to "where the wicked cease from troubling, and the weary are at rest."

During these five weeks, the exercises of the college had gone on without interruption, through the kind offices of the Rev. Mr. Riley, J. Wistar Simpson, Esq., S. R. Todd, Jr., W. W. Kennedy, and Miss Janie Kilgore, who, either together or in turn, had attended to the exercises of all the classes.

But an extra United States Court had been called for August, and every interest in that county was in such a chaotic condition, that the writer thought it due, both to himself and the college, for him to withdraw.

As to the United States Court, there had been silence the most profound, as to his "case," ever since his discharge, under bail, in Charleston, May 3d, 1872.

CHAPTER ELEVEN

☆ ☆ ☆ ☆

Recent Reconstruction

The details so far recorded, are those which grew out of the political persecution in Laurens County alone. In all the other counties where the writ of *habeas corpus* had been so arbitrarily suspended, the same reign of terror prevailed, and the trampling in the dust of all rights, social as well as civil.

In York County particularly, tales of horror are yet to be told, well calculated to mantle with shame the brow of any honest supporter of the present Administration. There the brute Merrill, holding a commission in the United States army, and backed by bayonets, was allowed unrestricted license to bully, oppress and degrade a defenceless people for months together. An inordinate greed for money, and a Nero-like delight in human torture, were, too evidently, the predominating characteristics of *this* "Major in the United States Infantry." None of the sanctities of *Home* – Anglo-Saxon in its name and institution – none of the safeguards of character – unimpeachable for honor and integrity – not even the sacredness of the pulpit, were any obstacles to his petty tyranny. Of his two "Assistant United States Marshals," it is enough to say, that one of them acted as Jack Ketch in the judicial murder of Mrs. Suratt, and the other was a congenial comrade of his.

But these tales must be told by some of the sufferers

themselves. They owe it to posterity to publish to the world what befell our down-trodden State under the infamous "Ku Klux" and "Enforcement" Acts.

Four years have rolled around since the occurrences detailed in the last chapter, and time has brought about some of his revenges.

The black Ku-Klux cloud has disappeared beyond our horizon, and the infamous Merrill, after following it to the *other* Dahomey, Louisiana, now finds himself called upon to account for some of his ill-gotten gains, before an investigating committee of Congress.

Joe Crews, equally infamous in Laurens, has gone to *his* final account. One morning, in the summer of 1875, he started very early from Laurens, in his buggy; was waylaid at a small creek, some four miles from the village; and was brought back, with six buckshot in different parts of his body. He lingered for a few days – died – and *was buried.*

No political significance is given to this horrid assassination, as he had long been shorn of all power from the withdrawal of all United States garrisons from Laurens. Public opinion has settled down into the conviction, that it was merely an act of private revenge, most probably at the hands of some of his own party – some of the same dregs to which he appropriately belonged. He was only of the scum, brought to the surface, in the boiling of the political cauldron, and it is astonishing how soon his memory has rotted.

But the old "State" is still "prostrate." The incubus of the ballot, in the hands of her former slaves, and manipulated by unscrupulous, and thieving carpet-baggers, still holds the true *citizen* of the State helpless, and almost hopeless.

In 1870, the first effort was made at political conciliation, by uniting upon Judge Carpenter, at that time regarded as trustworthy, in opposition to Scott, who had been nominated by the extreme Radicals, for a second term as Governor.

The result was a defeat by over thirty thousand! To show what kind of material we have to contend with in these carpet-baggers, it is only necessary to cite this single case of Carpenter. He was nominated by a "bolting faction" of his party, who made pretensions of contending for "honest government." Carpenter himself was loud and vehement in denouncing the abuses under the Scott administration, and the Conservative party rallied to his support with great unanimity.

Now, in this canvass of 1876, Carpenter is the acknowledged leader of the Whipper, Moses, and Elliott faction – the very worst of the band he was pledged to bring to grief.

In 1872, Tomlinson, who seems really to be the least objectionable of the fraternity, was selected to oppose the notorious F. J. Moses, the younger. In this case also, Tomlinson was the nominee of a party of "Bolters," and the Conservatives put forth their whole strength in his behalf. But the defeat was equally decisive.

Again, in 1874, a third attempt of the same kind was made, in the nomination of Judge Green, a *native* Republican, in opposition to Chamberlain, the regular nominee of the Radical party; and this time the majority was reduced to some ten thousand.

In this Centennial campaign of 1876, the Conservatives seem no longer disposed to conciliate and compromise, by selecting the less of two evils, held out by the opposite party, but to make "straight-out" Democratic nominations. They have faithfully tried the compromise policy for three successive administrations, and have signally failed in accomplishing any good. Now, they propose to reverse the experiment, and to invite all friends of good government, of whatever party, "race, or previous condition," to come over to their platform, and join in one earnest effort to redeem the State.

The experiment has already been carried out to a successful issue in Mississippi and Arkansas, and why may not these happy results be also felt in South Carolina? To any one with the wish and capacity to appreciate her present condition, no blacker picture could be drawn of any government in Christendom. Scott left the Treasury unbarred, but there was some pretension to honesty and decency, in all the glaring rascality of his administration. But the spend-thrift thief, Moses, threw the Treasury doors wide open, and bribery and corruption were organized into a fixed department of the government, under his rule. The remnants of the Treasury were plundered in the broad light of day, and the votes of the Legislature had their fixed market value, according to the importance of the measure to be passed, and the offices to be filled. Even the seat in the United States Senate, once filled by our Calhoun, was notoriously put up to the highest bidder, and one Patterson, a refugee from Pennsylvania, won it through his henchman, Worthington, a stranger in a strange land.

Such was the infamous record of the Moses administration, that his own party, bad as it was, had to repudiate him. To keep up even the semblance of decency, they were forced to adopt pledges of future reform, in the last canvass – mere *brutum fulmen* – to be entirely ignored as soon as their lease of power should be renewed. But the standard bearer, D. H. Chamberlain, had sagacity enough to see that their party had well nigh run its course. The very small majority, comparatively, by which he had been elected, and the case of Mississippi so suddenly and completely redeemed, opened his eyes fully to the feeble tenure by which he himself held his office.

He, therefore, deliberately adopted the role of Reformer. The sham platform erected by his party gave him a plausible pretext, and his insidious use of the English language in all his public documents, gave strong hopes of sincerity and wise statesmanship. In view of these, and some demonstrations of decision and firmness in carrying out his "reform-measures," the Conservatives of the State were disposed to rally most earnestly to his support. In doing so they had to ignore the greater part of this man's political career. A mere adventurer from Massachusetts, he had turned up, soon after the war, on one of the Sea Islands, near Charleston, where his violent counsels to the Freedmen, as to the vindictive course towards their former masters, had exasperated the native citizens against him, and thus made him one of the shining lights of Radicalism. His legal attainments, unquestionably great, soon brought him prominently before the Freedman's Bureau, and at the Reconstruction Constitutional Convention, he was selected as Attorney-General, under the first, or Scott administration. The State Treasury was then virgin soil for the Radical spoiler, and the havoc they made of the time-honored name and credit of the State, has already been fully delineated in these pages.

Chamberlain, as Attorney-General, was, *ex-officio,* a member of the Financial Board, and, whether he participated or not, he must, evidently, have been cognizant of all these enormous frauds by which the Treasury was so soon and so completely depleted. So far from any official denunciation of the course of his associates, we find him really upholding them. In Scott's canvass for re-election, Chamberlain took the stump, and, by an array of figures, attempted to prove that what are now known as the "Kimpton frauds," were the highest strokes of financial diplomacy.

Although all these antecedents were fresh in the memories of our tortured people, yet, the fact that a Radical Governor should talk kindly of the whites, and actually condescend to promise them some "Reforms," touched their hearts, and led them to try, most earnestly, to forget the past. Our newspapers were filled with eulogiums on his wise statesmanship and Roman firmness. Our most distinguished citizens were open in their official calls and conferences at the Executive office, and our Literary Institutions were vying with one another in calling on him for addresses at their scholastic anniversaries.

What stronger proofs are needed of the hopeless condition of a once proud people, than such acts as these – thus taking to their bosoms, and cheering to the echo, a Governor from Massachusetts who had only promised not to steal himself, and to use every effort to put a stop to the stealings of his friends!

Whether these promises and protestations were sincere or not, it became evident that he could not control his party, and that the course of the State was steadily downward. The Legislature, still lavish in expenditure, prolonged its two sessions to an average of four months each, instead of the four weeks promised. The tax bill and the appropriation bill, those vital subjects of legislation, were characterized by that wastefulness and extravagance which would have shocked our fathers in the palmiest days of prosperity. But, above all, this party made an exhibition of their utter disregard to anything like decency, in attempting to elevate to the Bench, by the votes of a large majority, two of the most corrupt scoundrels from the lowest of their own ranks – Ex-Governor Frank Moses and *General* Bill Whipper! Frank Moses had gone into bankruptcy, immediately after leaving the gubernatorial chair, which he had so notoriously disgraced, even as Scott's successor. He had become the veriest social outcast, and had no money to purchase votes, unless his more prudent father had hoarded for him some of his ill-gotten gains. The negro, Whipper, had long since gambled away all his stealings; and Attorney-General Melton had published, over his official signature, that he had not brought action against him for some large embezzlement because he was notoriously insolvent.

The Radical majority in the Legislature, therefore, did not even have the excuse of *bribery,* in making these creatures "Judges of the Circuit Court." The only solution of their course must be, that they intended this action as an open defiance to Governor Chamberlain, and to the moral sense of the whole State. They had the *power,* and they were determined to show that they could and would use this power as they pleased.

Probably no single act of the party in power has ever so thoroughly aroused our people to a more full appreciation of their degradation, and to the imminent danger which threatened even their civilization. Indignation meetings were, simultaneously, called all over the State, and the unanimous sentiment of these meetings has been, that this crowning outrage *shall never be consummated.*

Bill Whipper's circuit was to have embraced the Commercial Emporium of the State, and the staid old city was electrified in every fibre. She knew that upon the proper interpretation and enforcement of the law, depended, not only her commercial

prosperity, but the lives and property of her citizens. She knew
that this ignorant negro was scarcely fit to be admitted to a gentleman's kitchen, and her resolve was at once taken. Her utterances
were not loud, but deep, and portended a storm. It requires no
prophet, nor the son of a prophet, to announce, that this creature
will *never* take his seat on the Bench in Charleston. The time,
fixed by law, for a new judge to take his seat is in August, and
the matter must be postponed till then. Governor Chamberlain
has done all in his power to stay the evil by refusing to sign the
commissions of both of them, but they do not regard this as any
final action.

Moses' Circuit was to have included Sumter, where he
has been fully known from his earliest infancy. The full length
portrait drawn of him by his own neighbors would entitle him to
a conspicuous place in any future illustrated edition of Dante's
Inferno.

This spontaneous uprising of a whole people, goaded
almost to desperation by this outrage on all law, order, and civilization itself, deliberately perpetrated by the Radical party, "met
and sitting in General Assembly," for a time seemed to have
inspired some awe in their reckless ranks. But no serious effort
has been made to undo the mischief. They have "thrown one tub
to the whale," in the impeachment and conviction of one of their
imbecile judges, whose term was about to expire, and whose
successor had already been elected. Montgomery Moses, uncle
of Frank, and brother of Chief Justice Franklin J. Moses, was the
unfortunate victim selected. He belonged to that class of the judiciary familiarly called "old grannies," and was equally worthless
and harmless. His chief trouble seemed to have been impe-
cuniosity, and when he attempted to imitate the modern South
Carolina office-holder in "pickings and stealings," he bungled so
much that his tracks could be distinctly traced. He kept up some
semblance to honesty by *borrowing* from funds in charge of the
court, without any intention of returning the same; and this so
disgusted his brigand associates, that the whole pack turned upon
him, when they found they were expected to do *something.*

It was a clear illustration of Judge Butler's story of the bully, who, when kicked and cuffed about by men whom he had insulted, declared that he *could* whip somebody, and went home *and whipped his wife.*

CHAPTER TWELVE

☆　☆　☆　☆

Centennial Sentiments

If there is any truth in the old adage, that "the darkest hour always precedes the dawn," then may South Carolina now begin to indulge some hope. She has been brought low – very low – and even in the eyes of those who so bitterly condemned her for inaugurating Secession, her punishment must seem out of all proportion to her offense. The sufferings and atrocities of those four long years of war – beginning with the fall of Port Royal, and ending with the burning of Columbia – are yet to be written, with all their terrible details. Her property in slaves, which constituted the great bulk of her wealth, and which had descended from father to son for more than two centuries, was made to vanish into thin air by the breath of a proclamation. But worse than this, than these, than all, are her writhings under the humiliation, the spoliation, and the unremitting efforts at degradation, for the last ten years. Military rule, backed by an unscrupulous majority in Congress, occasioned forebodings of evil, the most fearful; but what pen can adequately describe the reality?

A sovereign State trampled in the dust, with the bayonet of the conqueror ever at her throat, is a fit tableau of – Reconstruction!

But if "the mills of the gods grind slowly, they grind exceeding fine." In very many cases there would be "no answer" to the long roll-call of her oppressors; and time is still busy in un-masking the chief agents in this horrid drama, in all their true colors and deformity.

Take the President of this great Republic himself. Ele-vated to a position where he might have made a name for him-self, for all time to come, as "saviour of his country," he has demonstrated that he has never had the intellect, nor the soul of the statesman or patriot. He cared nothing for his country, and his only care for the Republican party was, through it, to secure for himself an indefinite lease of power. It was a matter of indiffer-ence to him how the success of this party was to be secured, and what means might be resorted to. Whether the rights of individu-als, of whole communities, or of sovereign States were to be sacrificed, it gave him no concern. Success, at any and every cost, has been his watchword from the first to the last.

And the most mortifying fact to every American is, that an inordinate greed for gold has been the governing motive through his whole administration. The head being thus corrupt, can the student of history wonder at the wide-spread demoraliza-tion of the whole body politic, for the last eight years at least?

A hurling from power seems hardly a sufficient retribu-tion for the imprint of *Grantism* on our institutions in these de-generate days. He has prostituted his high office to the undermin-ing of the great political fabric of the fathers; to trampling on the time-honored rights of the great Anglo-Saxon race; and even to protecting and shielding official rapacity and dishonesty, when about to be exposed to an indignant people.

There was something grand in the gigantic strides of the first of all the Cæsars, when grasping for power; but the equally gigantic strides of this modern imitator have been made in pur-suit of – the almighty dollar! With the change of a single word, we, too, might adopt the indignant denunciation of Cato, in these burning words:

> "Oh, Portius, is there not some chosen curse,
> Some hidden thunder, in the stores of Heaven,

Red with uncommon wrath, to blast the wretch
Who owes his (*money*) to his country's ruin!"

At one time the approach of the centennial year seemed to have been the harbinger to the "dawn." Certainly hopes were inspired in bosoms long estranged from any emotion of the kind, and some indications of fraternal feelings began to develop. The review of the scenes and events of the first "great rebellion" on this continent seemed to have opened the Northern mind to a new light, and to have inspired their breasts with a charity equally new.

They began to question one another whether these Southern brethren, however mistaken, may not have been actuated by the same sense of right, and resistance to wrongs, which characterized the fathers in 1776. From their standpoint may not these brethren have regarded their liberty, based, as they deemed it to be, upon their ideas of States' Rights and State Sovereignty, as having been as much imperilled at the later date as in "the times that tried men's souls"? Would not these Northern brethren, in the same circumstances, have acted precisely as they did?

These wholesome questions began to be freely asked and considered, and promised to bring forth peaceable fruits. Such terms as *"Wicked Rebellion,"* "Rule or Ruin Policy," and a long list of ugly words engrafted upon their vernacular, by a life-long discussion of slavery, began gradually to fall into disuse. The questions formerly at issue began to lose their *moral* character, and to be viewed in their more appropriate *political* aspect. A great point was gained, when they began to utter the charitable sentiment, "Well, we are bound to admit that they *thought they were right.*"

In the case of South Carolina, particularly, public opinion began to tone down wonderfully. This review brought her prominently forward as one of the leading Colonies of the "Old Thirteen." Though the favorite Colony of the Crown, her magnanimity in so promptly throwing herself on the side of her oppressed sisters was still conspicuous after the lapse of an hundred years.

Her lavish expenditure of blood and treasure in the great cause she had espoused, was calculated to arouse sentiments of veneration and gratitude, particularly on the part of those younger sisters who had become prosperous and great under the very "independence" to which she had so largely contributed.

Even her old ally Massachusetts, seemed to have been drawn very near to her once more. These ancient Commonwealths have long been regarded as representatives of their respective sections. Gradually, from viewing the same objects from opposite standpoints, they had been driven very far apart – in fact to opposite points of the diameter. The first great obstruction between them was the "tariff question," and Massachusetts being on the side of it nearest the sun, could see nothing in it but what was bright, wholesome and life-giving, while South Carolina, from her cheerless side, saw all that was gloomy, impoverishing and destructive. This, though at one time so threatening, suddenly dissolved into empty gas before some big, swelling words of Nullification.

But there was another mutual eclipse, and though the obstacle this time was at first no bigger than a man's hand, it gradually developed into proportions the most portentous and awe-inspiring. This time *South Carolina* was on the sunny side, and she could only see in the clear beneficent light of slavery an institution recognized by God Himself, under both dispensations, and guaranteed by the fundamental law of the land.

From *her* standpoint, Massachusetts could only see blackness of darkness, imperfectly veiling "the sum of all villainies," and the "ragged edges of despair" around the sulphurous pits. Gunpowder, not gas, was now the word, and, unfortunately for the country, rifles of the most varied patterns were manufactured in the largest abundance on her soil. After some preliminary skirmishing in Kansas and Nebraska, and afterwards in the "John Brown Raid," the grand crashing came at last, resulting in an explosion which shook the Continent to its foundations.

However terrible the catastrophe, the obstacle was gone forever, and now that the turmoil and din are over, and the smoke almost blown away, these grim old antagonists can look one another once more in the face, and to their mutual surprise they began to see lineaments of real brotherhood. Each seemed almost ready to acknowledge that the same spirit – the spirit of the olden time – has all along been actuating them both, and had their standpoints been interchanged, each might have acted the part of the other.

At any rate, Massachusetts did not regard her programme for the grand centennial celebrations of her Concord, Lexington, and, particularly, of her Bunker Hill, complete, until she had assigned a conspicuous place to the old Palmetto State.

Armed men, from Charleston, were received by the citizens and soldiers of Boston, with the highest consideration and enthusiasm. The "citizen soldiers" of our "Washington Light Infantry," were welcomed, even at the railroad depot, by such a crowd as they had never seen before. At first they were a little nervous, not knowing what spirit might actuate this vast assembly; but, when a wide passage was spontaneously made for them through its very midst, and hats were waved, and cheers were given, as from one throat, they then *felt* what it all meant; and many a manly eye was seen to swim in tears. All along their march the side-walks were crowded by eager spectators, and the beauty as well as the "solid men" of this old metropolis turned out, in full force, to cheer and welcome them. Bouquets, oranges, bananas, etc., came flying fast from fair hands, which, those expert at the base ball, were not slow in catching and storing away. The only criticism on this showering of favors was, that the most soldierly-looking of the company received more than their due proportion.

The participants themselves have already given the public glowing accounts of this ever-to-be-remembered visit. From the first moment they touched the soil of Massachusetts, to the hour of their departure, the most cordial welcome, the most hearty greetings, the most generous hospitality, and the highest consideration awaited them; even to the "post of honor," on the day of the Bunker Hill pageant. How, then, could they feel like "strangers, in a strange land"? It was a *home* reception, and they were proud to feel at home. And, when they heard the patriotic, liberal sentiments of Gen. Bartlett and others of these Northern men, responded to by the ex-Confederate, Gen. Fitz Hugh Lee – who was cheered to the echo by enthusiastic crowds – is to be wondered at, that they should, for the time, forget all about State lines, and only remember their country, their *whole* country, and nothing but their country?

The tidings from Bunker Hill soon spread over the land, and produced a profound impression; and the magnanimous, whole-souled sentiments there uttered found a response in every generous bosom. It was seen that even extremists could meet at the graves of their revolutionary sires; could there look one another in the eye, and find that they were brethren after all. And if Massachusetts and South Carolina could so easily and heartily coalesce, who would dare, thereafter, to preach the "Gospel of Hate"?

Alas, for our unhappy land! This "dawn," so auspiciously heralded in by the centennial era, is now suddenly overcast in gloom.

Party spirit, and, worst of all, *sectional* party spirit, seems now stronger than patriotism; and the call of the mere political party leader more potent than the voice of the Christian statesman.

Already, in the halls of Congress, have those leaders stirred up a war of words to check this tidal wave of good feeling and reconciliation, so opposed to their selfish party interests, and to open afresh the wounds, just beginning to heal.

From the beginning the "father of his country" warned his fellow-citizens, and their posterity, against causing party lines to coincide with geographical lines; and intelligent foreign writers have pointed to this deadly sectional hate, thus engendered, as the hidden rock on which our glorious institutions are yet to founder.

Will these reckless political leaders succeed in carrying out their selfish schemes?

Is there common sense enough in the country to see through the transparent purposes of these political brawlers?

Is there patriotism enough in the country to postpone mere party triumph to the glory of the Reunited States?

As the once famous "Tom" Ritchie used to say, in days of yore,

"Nous verrons."

PART TWO:
After Hampton

POSTSCRIPT ONE

☆ ☆ ☆ ☆

Hampton's Campaign

The foregoing chapter was intended as the last of this "little book," but the financial embarrassments and business stagnation with our selected publisher were such, that our MS. has been lying quietly by us for more than a year, with the hope of finding a new one.

In the meantime, history has been progressing, and startling events have developed material enough for a much larger book, and one of a very different character. The centennial year has come and gone; the exciting, critical and astounding Presidential election has given a new and unique chapter to American politics; and the dark cloud, which has so long brooded over our State, has suddenly been rifted, and Wade Hampton is Governor of South Carolina!

These events, closely linked together as they have been, are on too magnificent a scale for mere human agency; and South Carolina has had her "Thanksgiving Day" for this signal deliverance from more than Egyptian bondage.

But we must proceed in some order; necessarily condensing into a brief abstract, subjects which may yet call forth volumes.

The grand Centennial Exposition at Philadelphia was, in every sense, worthy of the occasion, and its success has surpassed the wildest dreams of its most sanguine advocates. It has been national in its character, and its influence for good will tell on all our people for all time to come. Representatives from every part of our broad land were brought into familiar contact for weeks and months together, and ties were renewed between those great families of States which had been weakened by long estrangement, and which the great civil war had well nigh sundered. As nearly all the peoples of the earth were represented there, if not by personal representatives, yet by specimens of their skill, art and industries, the favorable occasion served greatly to enlarge our views; to throw down and uproot the prejudices of centuries, and to show that, for cultivated skill, and enterprising industry, "the field is the world."

The Presidential election, too, is much too grave a theme to be discussed in mere postscript chapters. Forty millions of people, distributed over thirty-eight different States, have as much interest in that wild contest, and its anomalous close, as the writer has, and he may well leave the discussion for abler pens, and wiser heads. His "Voice," were he to attempt it, would be like the war-cry of the disembodied Greeks, at the approach of Æneas.

This much may be allowed: The "counting in" of President Hayes was the climax in a series of bold steps in political "progress," for which the party now in power has acquired a world-wide notoriety. Starting in 1860 as a strictly sectional party, it defied and brought on a strictly sectional war. Since then it has exercised a sectional domination, on which all the arbitrary powers of the Old World have gazed with amazement. It has created "States" out of ancient commonwealths, with constitutions framed at its own bidding, and utterly repugnant to those governed. It has manipulated the sacred right of the "ballot" to suit its own purposes: and, now that this ballot has made one effort at independent action, this party unblushingly reverses its decisions, by changing sixteen electoral votes to secure a majority of one! This, too, in the face of a popular majority of more than 300,000! As a single, original act of usurpation, its frightful enormity would have shocked the whole American people; but being, as it is, the last of a series, it seems to be viewed in different lights, according as the eye has or has not become accustomed to startling visions.

There was one decision by this mighty vote, however, which even this reckless party could not ignore. Throughout the length and breadth of the land it was proclaimed, in thunder tones, that this vile oppression of American citizens MUST cease! Accordingly, one of the first acts of the Hayes Administration, was to withdraw Federal bayonets from the legislative halls of sovereign States, and thus make way for State officers, selected by their own people. Thus the Governors elected by the people were allowed to take their seats; and Louisiana hailed her Nicholls as Chief Magistrate, and South Carolina, her Wade Hampton!

Mr. Hayes accomplished as much for us, in this deliverance, as Tilden himself could have done, and without that hue and cry which would have followed the action of a Democratic Executive. So that Hayes' inauguration has proved a blessing in disguise to our down-trodden people, and we certainly owe him no grudge.

In a succinct resumé of the memorable events of 1876, it would delight the writer to linger long around Fort Moultrie, and give some of the details of the centennial celebration of South Carolina's Thermopylæ. Here her *four* hundred, without hope of retreat, held their station in what General Charles Lee called a "slaughter-pen," fully determined to do or die. They did not suffer the fate of Sparta's *three* hundred, but, on the contrary, gradually drove back the combined fleet of the "Mistress of the Sea." Are they to be honored by their posterity the less on this account?

In the midst of desponding fears, and while groaning under grievous wrongs, the ancient city of Charleston put on her gala dress, and invited the whole country to a participation in this glorying in the past. The whole State responded, because this great battle, fought before the "Declaration," was *her* first act of sovereignty and independence. Whatever her present sufferings and attempted degradation, the past was secure, and belonged to her and her children.

Massachusetts responded nobly to the call, and from under the shadow of Bunker Hill monument, the choice of her military companies were sent to give the right hand of fellowship, and to participate fully in all the honors of the occasion. The grand ovation given our military the year before, in sight of Bunker Hill, could not be reciprocated in our impoverished condition, but the same spirit and the same heart were there.

In the beautiful "Moultrie Monument," which now adorns White Point Garden, in Charleston, and from her Battery looks out upon Sullivan's Island and old ocean, Boston has an undivided share contributed with all the frankness of manly and Christian chivalry.

But while these exhibitions of our higher and nobler nature were thus called forth by memories of the past, the grim demon of hate, with all its relentless venom, was still abroad in the land. The cue given by politicians of the Blaine school, in Congress, was taken up by unscrupulous demagogues at widely separated points, in the heated Presidential contest then going on. The "bloody shirt" was waved most furiously, particularly in the Northwest, and any Southern "outrage" was eagerly watched for to rekindle the failing embers. The local incendiaries, particularly the emissaries of the carpet-bag authorities, were most active in fomenting a strife of races.

In South Carolina they thought they had made a case, in what they were pleased to call the "Hamburg Horror." Hamburg had once been a thriving business mart, but the railroad had sapped it of all prosperity. The buildings had been almost wholly abandoned by the whites, and, of course, they became the harbors for dissolute and vagrant negroes, and a sure retreat for escaped convicts from every part of the State. The charter being still in existence, they had the whole municipal control. This was regarded by the Radical authorities as the most combustible point in the State, and arms were furnished, and emissaries sent among them to stir up trouble. Need we go on to the sequel so often repeated among our long-suffering people?

Negroes, with arms in their hands, offer some insults and indignities to high-spirited young men. This, of course, is resented. Others flock to the scene, the lines are drawn, and the negroes retire to fortify themselves in an abandoned building. The first blood shed was that of a white man; shot through the head, while standing with his comrades on the defensive. This highly exasperated the whole community, far and near; the more restless spirits were soon on the ground, and in the lead, and that night the negroes were made to suffer.

The telegraph wires throughout the land were busy all the next day, in flashing this terrible "outrage" to the remotest hamlet. Fortunately for the cause of truth, the Circuit Court was soon after in session, and those who were denounced as the "bloody rioters," voluntarily gave themselves up, and demanded a trial, even before a Radical Judge. But it was no part of the programme to have the *truth* come out, so the whole matter was postponed to the next court, *and they never have been tried!*

The next horror was the "Ellenton Riots," inspired by the same parties, and with the same objects in view. A white woman had been most inhumanly assaulted and maltreated by a negro, who was afterwards recognized by a little child. An arrest was, of course, attempted, but in due course of law, yet, such was the spirit then among the negroes, that they felt bound to aid one of their own number, against the whites, right or wrong. Small bodies uniting became formidable in their proportions, and the organizations on the part of the whites, also greatly exceeded the usual *"posse comitatus."* The feeling spread from neighborhood to neighborhood, and from community to community, till that whole section of country seemed to be under arms. Just at the crisis, threatening an immediate conflict, a detachment of United States soldiers appeared on the ground, and by their intervention both sides agreed to disband and go home quietly.

The parties arrested, on the part of the whites (there were none on the part of the blacks), also insisted on immediate trial, but they, too, were "postponed."

However, early in the present year, their case *has* been heard. Corbin, familiarly called "Ku-Klux Korbin," the malignant United States District Attorney, had selected those he regarded as the worst cases on the list, had filled all the negro boarding-houses in Charleston with an unlimited number of colored "witnesses," had manipulated the juries, both grand and petit; and yet, after all his efforts in their trial, he could only secure a "mistrial" – jury failing to agree!

Of course, that settled the whole matter, and we will hear no more of the "Ellenton Rioters," in the courts at least.

But these offsets from "Centennial fraternizing," have led us to anticipate the regular course of events.

Chamberlain was still playing his bold game of apparently conciliating a people whom he both hated and feared, and, at the same time, retaining the confidence and control of his own party. In the face of the election of Moses and Whipper to the bench, he had positively refused to commission them. About the same time, and in allusion to this election, he had said, in response to an invitation to the anniversary of the New England Society, in Charleston, that "the civilization of both the Hugenot and Cavalier was in imminent danger." He had denounced Elliott, his colored Attorney-General, in the most bitter and opprobrious terms; and, in those pen-pictures, in which he so eminently excels, was representing himself as in the van of "Reform," sword drawn, and scabbard thrown away! And our confiding people were disposed to believe him, attributing his villainous appointments and conniving with thieves and rogues, to *necessity,* in carrying out his policy! Even in May, 1876, when the first Democratic Convention met, he had the trembling confidence of a majority of the members. Col. M. C. Butler and Gen. Gary, both from Edgefield, denounced him and his policy in no measured terms, and insisted, even then, on a "straightout" Democratic nomination for State officers; but the majority were still hoping for "Reform" from the great High Priest of Radicalism. The summer passed over, the bomb-shells of "Hamburg" and "Ellenton" had been exploded, the military grip on the State was becoming stronger and tighter, and all "Reform" was still in abeyance. The question now was, must the old State, Samson-like, in being both captive and blind, but "make sport" in the presence of her exulting enemies, her own people aiding and abetting?

A very different spirit prevailed in the Democratic Convention which re-assembled in August. The conviction was now forced upon her citizens, that if South Carolina was ever to be redeemed, it was to be done by her own people, under their own leaders. All temporizing and compromising was then boldly thrown aside. The Sate was ranged squarely under the Democratic banner, and her own sons, well tried and true, were nominated for her highest offices.

This, of course, was an immediate checkmate to Chamberlain's deep-laid and long-plotted scheme. But, in the emergency he was – *himself!* With a reckless boldness which his friends have dignified with the name of courage, but which seems more appropriate to the character of the detected assassin, he, at once, threw off the mask, and openly took his stand at the head of the worst elements of his party. At the Radical Convention, soon after assembled, he claimed and received their nomination, as their acknowledged chief, and, arm-in-arm with *Elliott*, he deposited his vote, nominating the latter for reelection.

The nomination of Gen. Wade Hampton for Governor, sent a thrill like electricity through the State, and revived hopes long drooping and well nigh dead. The mere possibility of having this favorite son of the State at the head of affairs, stirred the hearts of all her people, and awakened emotions of patriotism long deemed crushed out.

Hampton, himself, seemed inspired for the occasion. Busily occupied in efforts to recover something from the ruins of his once magnificent estates, he at once threw aside all private matters, and boldly entered upon a campaign unequalled in the annals of Republics. All the State officers were arrayed against him, with their "election machinery" arranged and perfected through a whole decade of unbroken success. The Radical State census called for more than 30,000 majority of colored votes. The administration at Washington was ready and anxious to furnish all the resources of the army and navy to uphold this nondescript government, in order to secure the electoral vote of the State, in the exceedingly close contest, then going on, for President of the United States.

This state of things would have appalled any personal aspirant for office; but Hampton seems, from the first, to have thrown aside the personal, and to have regarded himself as the embodiment of the "Forlorn Hope" of South Carolina. All public gatherings, all strife of words, and particularly all public speaking were averse to his natural tastes; but, with a self-sacrifice worthy the cause, he plunged headlong into the midst of all these, and with a consciousness that there could be no respite till the end.

Beginning in the mountains, where the news of his nomination first reached him, he made appointments to meet his constituents, successively, at all the important points of the State, from the mountains to the sea-board. His opponents, and particularly Chamberlain, were invited to meet him at all these places, with an assurance of protection and safe conduct. These appointments left but few intervals for "rest days," through the whole campaign, and, what is very remarkable, he never failed to be present, and, personally, to address his fellow-citizens. The very elements seemed to favor him, for no occasion was marred by foul weather, and all the rains occurred in the intervals of his appointments.

Within sight of those everlasting hills, which look down upon the memorable battle-fields of "Cow-pens" and "King's Mountain," he first raised his clarion voice for Redemption and Home Rule. An enthusiasm was at once enkindled, which drew out unprecedented crowds to his first appointment. It was feared that this unanimity would be confined to that section of the State – always Democratic, and, comparatively exempt from the heel of the oppressor. But as Hampton approached the middle country, the crowds became even greater, and the enthusiasm almost reached delirium. Each county had one or more of its "Hampton's Days," and each of these "days" vied with its predecessor, not only in numbers, but in decorations and pageantry.

There was one potent influence in inspiring and urging forward this wild excitement and jubilant greeting, which Hampton never failed to acknowledge publicly, and with choking gratitude, – and that was the *women* of the State! They prepared the way for him, wherever he went, for he found them everywhere the same. However gloomy and despondent their husbands and brothers may have become, *they* had never "despaired of the Republic," but were as unyielding and defiant, even in the darkest days of oppression, as when the Confederate flag waved over Fort Sumter, or on the hill-tops of Bull Run. The candid historian must record, that if it had not been for the women of the State, her early redemption from Radical rule would have been impossible, for Hampton himself has said as much.

It was the privilege of the writer to attend several of these "ovations," and he can assert that nothing like them had ever been witnessed in this State, even in her palmiest days. Before the war, she had always been so unanimous in Federal politics, that political campaigns were comparatively unknown, and no mere local contest had ever so stirred the public heart.

But where was Chamberlain all this while? Invitation after invitation had appeared in the papers, calling upon him to meet Hampton at some of these places most convenient to him, but he clung to his Executive hole in Columbia, sending forth his meshes, spider-like, all over the State, to entrap a hated people.

To thwart the growing enthusiasm, he naturally looked to the bayonet, which had placed him where he was, and still retained him there. He was most ardently desirous to have martial law proclaimed, but that was in the power of the President, and from the course of the Federal canvass, then going on, the President himself would have to plead a strong case. To force some such emergency, his counsellors inaugurated the "strike" among the half civilized blacks of the low country rice-fields, but under the "Peace Policy," inculcated by Hampton, all these efforts failed.

The only effect was to damage a few individuals, and to bring down untold want and suffering on these deluded creatures themselves.

He next thought of striking at the "chivalry" of the State, by calling for the disbanding and disarming of all the ride clubs, and volunteer military organizations throughout the State. By specious representations made to Washington, he *did* induce the President to issue a Proclamation to that effect.

It so happened that the writer was present when this was first announced to Hampton, which was on the great "Hampton Day," at Sumter C.H. The speaking was all over, and the General was quietly dining with a private party, at a friend's house. Sitting nearest his hostess, he was interrupted in the midst of a remark to her by the "telegraph boy," handing him a dispatch, with the request that he would read it at once. He did so, and quietly folding the note, he finished the remark he was making to Mrs. F., and no one would or did suppose, from his manner, that there was anything of importance in its contents. But when Col. Haskel requested him to throw it across the table, one glance from him brought out the exclamation: "Here it is, true enough! The President has disbanded all the white companies, and threatens us with martial law!" The countenances around the table wore very different expressions from Hampton's schooled features, and we could not but admire that Roman self-control so often manifested lately.

By his *advice,* which was as effective as a *ukase* from the Court of St. Petersburg, among the Russians, this order from Washington was promptly obeyed, and fully carried out, and Mr. Chamberlain was again checkmated.

It was an anomaly to see a late dashing "Lieutenant-General of Cavalry" so suddenly and so sternly acting the apostle of William Penn, in his peace policy; but South Carolina, at that time, witnessed that metamorphosis. And she, to-day, rejoices in a victory, unequalled in her annals, achieved by legal methods alone, and by tactics unqualifiedly *Quaker.* The truth is, there was not then, nor had there ever been in South Carolina, any one man who could have carried out that policy but General Hampton himself. Even John C. Calhoun would have signally failed. Hampton's war record had caused him to be regarded as the personification of the chivalry and manhood of the State, and when he counselled *yielding,* even General Gary had to subside.

POSTSCRIPT TWO

☆　☆　☆　☆

Redemption and Home Rule

The election came on, at last, and Chamberlain had his United States soldiers and marshals distributed throughout the State, to his entire satisfaction. But to the surprise of friend and foe, Wade Hampton had a clear majority of over twelve hundred votes! In the strong Radical precincts in Charleston, Colleton and Beaufort Counties, such untold frauds had been practiced that the most sanguine had begun to despair of success; and when it was found that the election was safe, in spite of all these frauds, the people rejoiced "with exceeding great joy." But the shout of triumph soon subsided, when that omnipotent Radical "Returning Board" was summoned to "canvass the votes." By the simple device of "counting out" the two counties of Laurens and Edgefield, which had gone Democratic by large majorities, it was attempted to reverse the result, and "count in" Chamberlain and his crew.

In vain did the Supreme Court attempt to restrain this Board, in its usurpation of power. After several attempts on the part of the court had been successfully foiled, an order of court was finally passed for them to bring all the election returns into court the next day. But that night, under the inspiration of Corbin, the Board formally declared Chamberlain and crew elected, issued the usual certificates, and then adjourned *sine die.*

A short time afterwards the court had them all arrested, imposed a fine of $1,500 each, and had them all committed to jail, in default of payment. But the notorious Judge Bond, of the U. S. Circuit Court, was soon on the ground, summoned by telegraph. He at once released them on writs of *habeas corpus,* at Chambers, and, not long afterwards, made their discharge final!

An expression had escaped from Hampton's heart, through his unguarded lips, which served to quiet all apprehensions as to the result. It was to the following effect: "The people of South Carolina have elected me Governor, and, by the Eternal God, I intend to be their Governor!"

The time for the convening of the Legislature now drew nigh, and all eyes were turned to Columbia to see which party would secure the supremacy. The same vote which had made Hampton Governor, secured a majority of the House of Representatives. There were senators enough holding over to give that body to the Radicals by a small majority.

A short time before the day of meeting, Chamberlain had procured an order from President Grant to have a Company of United States Infantry quartered in the State House. This was effected at midnight, and the next morning, the citizens found access to the halls of their fathers, debarred by armed sentinels wearing the United States uniform, and posted at every door!

On the day of the meeting of the Legislature, a large crowd of every color and condition was assembled on the open area, in front of the State House, and even the broad steps leading to the main doorway were crowded. The officer in command had announced that only those bearing certificates from the Returning Board could be admitted. The excitement became intense, until Hampton himself appeared on the steps. He had just been refused admittance, but was as calm as a summer's morning. He only uttered a few words, to the effect that the handful of United States soldiers before them represented a power it would be madness to resist. That he felt *that* place was not a proper one for him, and, therefore, was going to his office. His *advice* was, for all who felt as he did, to follow him down the street. As he advanced to the gate, the whole crowd silently melted away into a solemn procession, following his lead.

His Excellency's "office," was a suite of two rooms over one of the stores on Main street, and furnished as his room on the Campus had been in College days, excepting the cot bedstead.

The members elect had all been admitted into their hall, excepting the two delegations from Laurens and Edgefield. The Radical members were sworn in, and, although without a quorum, proceeded to organize by the election of Mackey, of Charleston, as Speaker. The Democratic members then withdrew to "Carolina Hall," and organized the true House of Representatives, by electing Gen. Wallace, of Union, their speaker. There were several defections from the Mackey to the Wallace House, which soon secured the constitutional quorum, beyond all cavil. As the admissions into the State House had gradually become more relaxed, Gen. Wallace privately informed his members that he intended to occupy the Speaker's chair, at the Capital, on the next adjournment of the Mackey House. This was quietly effected, Wallace occupying the chair, with all his members present. At his regular time, Mackey came in and demanded the chair, and, on being peremptorily refused, he ordered a common chair to be placed as near to Wallace as the impenetrability of matter would permit. Here he took his seat, and called his pretended House to order. Then was presented the unprecedented spectacle of two Houses of Representatives, organized and sitting in the same hall. The Radical House, almost exclusively colored, occupied the left of the Speaker, and the Democrats the right, separated by the broad middle aisle.

It was somewhat confusing to a spectator to listen to two calls for the "yeas and nays," going on simultaneously; but more so in a double debate, when there was a greater contest of lungs than brains. Yet all this continued for more than four days – day and night. The session of each succeeding day was resumed precisely at the moment of adjournment at the preceding day, keeping each speaker in his seat continuously. It was a question of endurance only; for, with the United States soldiers down stairs, and within easy call, there was no idea of *force*.

It was hard service for these gentlemen to be thus shut up with these unwashed "wards of the nation," sending forth a stifling, native perfume, when the piercing cold without prevented necessary ventilation. Sleeping, too, on dirty floors, each with a single blanket, would read well in a story of martyrdom, but their heads and frames ached nevertheless. In all this the negroes had the great advantage, as they were just in their element. The perfume served but to stimulate them to song and jollity, and a blanket big enough to cover the head was all that each needed. On the other hand, in eating and drinking, the whites had the incalculable advantage. While Sambo was munching his hard tack and cheese, he had to gaze wishfully on baskets and boxes of fruit and tempting viands furnished the other side, in profusion, by the rebel-sympathizing merchants of Columbia and Charleston.

Even then, accessions were made to the Wallace House, and, as each sable orator would make his speech, take the qualifying oath, and direct his steps to the "Right," he would be warmly welcomed to a goodly pile of apples, oranges, bananas, etc. After four days of such experience as this, Speaker Wallace was privately informed that an effort would be made to eject the delegations from Laurens and Edgefield, and, if resistance was made, the officer in command of the United States troops had orders to interfere in force. As this would bring on a direct collision with the General Government, of course, the question was settled very promptly. On motion, the Wallace House adjourned to their former hall, and this unique contest was ended, without bloodshed.

Not long after this, Chamberlain was "inaugurated" before a constitutional Senate and usurping House; Hampton also took the oath of office, in the open air, and in presence of the constitutional House, a minority of the Senate, and a large concourse of distinguished citizens. Soon after this, the whole Legislature, real and fictitious, adjourned *sine die*.

Hampton, after his inauguration, made a demand on Chamberlain for the Executive office, papers, etc., but as Chamberlain had this office, as well as his private residence, strictly guarded by U.S. troops, he sent back a peremptory refusal.

The Supreme Court had been reduced almost to a state of anarchy. The Chief Justice, still in doubt as to which would prove the winning side, in the Presidential contest, was vacillating and non-commital in all his official acts. In this condition of things, he was suddenly stricken down with paralysis, and soon afterwards was called to his final account. Associate Justice Willard had, from the first, set his face, like a flint, against all the revolutionary schemes and dishonest practices of his party, and was firm and immovable on the side of right and justice. *Ass.-* Justice Wright, the colored representative of this body, was everything in turn, and nothing at last. Agreeing to one decision when sober, and retracting when drunk, he has managed to forfeit all respect, even from the decent representatives of his own race.

The result of all their decisions was the recognition of the body presided over by General Wallace, as the true House of Representatives, and the legal election of the Democratic Executive officers. The election of Governor, was, of course, a question for the Legislature, and this had already been practically decided.

Hope was reviving in every faithful bosom, and the day of redemption seemed really drawing near. The old State pride began, once more to develop, as the prospect grew brighter of South Carolina again resuming her position among her sister States But this feeling was cruelly checked by the last official act of President Grant in her case, and a fitting climax to all his previous steps in military tyranny.

What was left of the chartered military companies of Charleston, under the lead of the "Washington Light Infantry" had agreed to celebrate Washington's Birthday (22d February), with all the show of military under their control. To aid in this patriotic demonstration the choice volunteer companies of Savannah and Augusta were invited to attend and participate. *But,* Chamberlain telegraphed the startling intelligence to Washington

City, and forthwith, there came an order from the War Department, peremptorily forbidding any such military display.

Comment is unnecessary.

Soon after followed the "counting in" of President Hayes, and his inauguration, which "followed hard upon." But those United States bayonets were still in the State House at Columbia, and Chamberlain was still daily riding to and from the Executive office, in his close carriage. After weeks of suspense had run into months, to the surprise of everybody, Hampton and Chamberlain were both invited to personal interviews with the President, and *at the same time.*

What passed at these interviews, which were separate, are State secrets, but what the public could ascertain was cheering enough to the friends Of Hampton. His journey to and from Washington was almost a continued ovation at the railroad stations along his route, and at Washington he was treated with the most distinguished consideration. His appearance, on his return, in spite of all his prudent reticence, showed that he now felt himself to be the master of the situation. Chamberlain, on the other hand, paid his visit "unknowing and unknown," as to the outside world, and came back with a head of the bulrush order.

Time alone will bring to light, if ever it is done, all that transpired at Washington during these weeks of intense anxiety. We could learn that several Congressmen from the South had ardently espoused the cause of Hampton, and were exerting all the influence they had in his behalf. Particularly Senator Gordon, of Georgia, who had, with all his heart, thrown himself into the contest, and was moving all in his power in behalf of South Carolina. No native son of hers could have shown a more lively interest in her redemption, and his eminent and self-sacrificing services will always be treasured in the memory of a grateful people.

Not long after Hampton's visit there was issued, from the War Department, an order for the United States Infantry, then in charge of the State House, by noon of a certain day to *march out,* and resume their old quarters at the garrison post. This was all –

but it was all we wanted. That little paper of some ten lines, ordering about two dozen United States enlisted men to march about half a mile, produced a mighty revolution, as peaceful as it was complete, and changed the status of our ancient Commonwealth for all time to come! The Federal bayonet was withdrawn from her throat, and she at once arose from her dust and ashes, and is, even now, putting on her beautiful garments. The whole monstrous fabric of radicalism, which the usurpers proudly thought securely pinned together by bayonets, for this generation at least, *in a moment* came toppling about their ears. The effect produced on this motley crowd was amusing enough to those who saw that their escape was impossible. Homeless and keeperless, they could find no shelter from the wrath to come!

A second demand from Hampton now promptly brought about the humiliating surrender of Executive office, archives, etc., and Chamberlain was soon after wholly absorbed in boxing up his elegant household furniture, for the steamer in Charleston. A day or two afterwards he followed these boxes himself – but *he will return.* As a culprit, he will yet have to stand before that altar of Justice he has dared so long and so often to defile with his unhallowed touch; and answer to charges of high crimes and misdemeanors, embracing conspiracies for purposes of fraud and *larceny.*

It required but little effort now for the incumbents to get possession of all the State offices, and soon the State was fully equipped for her new departure. After proclaiming a day of solemn Thanksgiving to Almighty God (which was generally and heartily observed), the Governor summoned the Legislature together in solemn form.

This time the inside of the State House presented a very different appearance from that of the preceding winter. After weeks of convict labor expended on her halls, they began to look as if fitted up for the reception of gentlemen.

In organizing, there was a little ripple of excitement in the Senate chamber, which was soon calmed by the wise course and admirable presence of mind of Col. W.D. Simpson, the new

Lieutenant-Governor. His predecessor, Gleaves, had requested, as a special favor, to be allowed to call the Senate to order, and then, from his seat as President, to lay aside all badges of office and retire gracefully. This was done; but a motion was then made for the formal inauguration of the new Lieutenant-Governor. Colonel Simpson saw that this would ignore all his past official acts, and, stepping forward he declared that no power on earth could force him to take the oath of office a second time. Then, without waiting for the formality of being conducted there by a committee, he boldly marched up and into the President's chair. There was some confusion, but by a few skillful rulings on points of order, he soon quieted matters, and had all the wheels of legislation running smoothly, before the gaping crowd around him could realize the brilliant *coup de-etat.*

In the Hall of Representatives, the old roll of the Wallace House was called, to the consternation of the Mackeyites, who found themselves occupying their former seats, but, this time as mere spectators. After the usual preliminary measures were acted on, still without noticing these uneasy legislators, the House quietly adjourned. After they had been sufficiently tried in this way, a resolution was introduced to admit the delegations from certain counties, on their purging themselves of contempt for the true House of Representatives, at its preceding session, by apologies the most humble; and earnestly begging pardon for the same. This was an edifying spectacle for the whole State, and well calculated to benefit the penitents themselves; though it was well known that their acquiescence was occasioned more by appeals from their pockets, than from their consciences.

Hamilton, a very shrewd and intelligent negro, from Beaufort, had been the first, publicly, to go over to the Wallace House the winter before. On this occasion he was in his glory, and his appeals for the "mourners to come forward, and seek pardon," were ludicrous enough. In some of the more obdurate cases, he would stand up with them in the aisle, as if he was their sponsor; while on others, he would imitate "the laying on of hands."

The whole delegation from Charleston, nineteen in number, were permanently excluded, on the ground *of fraud* in their election; and that old city has sent a full Democratic ticket in their stead – good men and true, – and some of her ablest and longest tried citizens.

On one ground and another, the seats of certain senators were vacated, and these were promptly filled by Democrats – the Radicals, as in Charleston, making no nominations. At last, the sudden disappearance of the notorious Whittemore, from that body, gave the Democrats the majority there also. Whittemore's seat was declared vacant, and a Democrat has been elected in his place also.

The most important action of this session of the Legislature, was the appointment of two able committees to sit during the recess. The first committee was to investigate the financial condition of the State, particularly her bonded debts. The second is to inquire into and bring to trial, all frauds, high crimes and misdemeanors perpetrated against the State, under Radical rule.[1]

It was this last measure that frightened Whittemore off, and has caused many others to depart abruptly. But it is no part of the committee's duties or purpose to drive the Radicals from the State. So far from it they are sending to the highways and hedges, and *compelling* them to come in. Their proceedings, of course, are private; but, from their success, thus far, and from the character of the tribunal, there is no doubt that their work will be thoroughly done.

Our narrative now closes in the midst of this most stupendous revolution, and one brought about by means, apparently, so inadequate. It was the result of prudence, caution and long-suffering patience – qualities in which South Carolina has but recently been indoctrinated – all guided by profound wisdom.

The grand result has given Hampton a name above every other name in the State, and has enthroned him in the hearts of all his true countrymen, and countrywomen too. But say to him,

1. See Appendix.

"Never had a people such a chief to follow!" and his answer would be promptly returned, "Never had a chief such a people to hold up his hands, and urge him forward *in his own way!*"

Neither is his fame confined by State lines. Such patriotism and statesmanship as he has recently illustrated, will captivate and impress all who can appreciate such rare qualities, always and everywhere.

Take the following tribute from Senator Bayard, than whom none stands higher, in this latitude, among living American statesmen. In an address delivered at Pimlico, he says:

"Few figures stand forth upon the canvas of history so eminent as that of John Hampden, the English country gentleman, whose monument records that, 'with great courage and consummate abilities, he began a noble opposition to an arbitrary court, in defence of the liberties of his country; supported them in Parliament, and died for them on the field!'

"And his compeer in virtue and ability, separated in date, by more than two centuries, but who will ever rank with him in history; whose constancy and sound judgment, whose intrepidity and self-control, have proved such a shield and buckler to his people, when beset by difficulties and dangers greater than even Hampden confronted, is to-day, supplied in our own land, in Wade Hampton, the planter of South Carolina!

"Hampden and Hampton! The names blend in sound, and in future time, 'Far on in summers that we shall not see,' they will be coupled in the lessons taught to inspire the youth of all lands with patriotic endeavor."

But it would be folly to claim this great success as the work of any one man. It can safely be asserted that from the inception of the political campaign to its glorious consummation, in the withdrawal of the United States troops from the State House, not one material blunder was made! This is more than can be attributed to any one mortal man, and Governor Hampton himself would cheerfully furnish a list of names, which would make an additional chapter necessary to this little book.

The unique and unprecedented contest between the "Wallace" and the "Mackey" House of Representatives called for qualifications of a rare order in the presiding officer, and Gen. W. H. Wallace proved himself to be the right man, in the right place. Had he proved weak, vacillating or even compromising, the whole scheme of reformation in the government might have failed. Though the body over which he presided was composed mainly of young and inexperienced members, yet his cool head, steady nerve and iron will, held them in constant check, and shaped their course with admirable tact. Those who witnessed the confusion, the turmoil and the provocations of those dark days, and nights, too, were at a loss which to admire most, the calm dignity with which these were overruled, or the consummate skill which led to final and complete success.

Probably a still more critical, though far less protracted task was assigned to the Lieutenant-Governor-elect. The State had known Col. W. D. Simpson as a highly gifted and very popular "citizen of the old school," but as wholly untried in parliamentary tactics. The Radical Senate – from the first recognized as legal by both parties – was about to begin its work at the called session. Gleaves, Chamberlain's Lieutenant-Governor, was easily induced to resign his seat as *ex-officio* President, on a pledge of immunity for some notorious penitentiary offence. But to the Senate, Col. Simpson was only the "so-called" Lieutenant-Governor. While they were wrangling over the difficulty in excited debate, mainly on the point of his taking the oath of office a second time, Governor Simpson, by one of those inspirations which so rarely occur in a life-time, at once settled the question by stepping up to the vacant chair and taking his seat, while boldly announcing that no human power could force him to repeat that oath. The mere magnetism of his presence and bearing seemed at once to bring order out of confusion. At any rate this was all that appeared to the outsiders; but there must have been much manipulating and adroit management to render this bold step so completely successful. This was the first official act of Governor Simpson; but before this, and all through the campaign, he had devoted his energies and all his powers to the cause so near his heart. In the Legislative struggle, which was really the crisis of the contest, Governor Hampton always found in Simpson and Wallace the Aaron and Hur, ever ready to hold up his hands when almost overwhelmed by the gravest responsibilities.

The writer can bear testimony to the indefatigable, self-sacrificing labors of the "Executive Committees" of the several counties. In addition to greater labor of the same character, the "State Executive Committee," at Columbia, were pre-eminently of the Governor's Council. Among these the noble figure of Col. A.C. Haskell stands very prominent. From his enviable character for spotless integrity and chivalric honor, he enjoyed the unstinted confidence of his chief, and the highest esteem of his fellow-laborers. His self-devotion to the great cause was only second to that of Hampton himself. When he called on the auxiliary clubs for additional work, he set them the example by working himself. When he advised Gen. Wallace to seize the Speaker's chair, he took his little blanket and slept on the dirty floor with the members. And at the following "called session," when the time for rewards had come, he declined every nomination for political position tendered him by his grateful fellow-citizens. He has won his country's plaudit, as her *chevalier sans peur et sans reproche!*

But we must never forget that the great contest was, mainly, a *legal* one, and the true champion in that fight was the gallant and gifted Gen. James Conner, of Charleston. Quietly, but with admirable tact, he prompted most of those moves on the political chess-board which so effectually checked all the skill and finesse of Chamberlain, the adroit but unprincipled Radical leader. The magnificent checkmate of 1876 having cleared the way before him, he is seeking, with rare modesty, to withdraw from public gaze into the shades of private life. But his State has appreciated his ability and devotion, and in her time of need will know where to look.

Gen. Johnson Hagood was another in this small group of constant and confidential counsellors, whose views exerted a controlling influence on measures of vital importance. Generally silent and unobtrusive, he was always found prompt and efficient when the occasion called for him. His opinions were eminently characterized by wisdom – if that is shown in clearness of perception, vigor as well as nice discrimination in judgment, coolness and firmness in deciding, and unflinching nerve in execution. Gov. Hampton was not long in recognizing these high traits, and his counsel was sought when many an older and more eloquent aspirant for leadership was passed by. Like true bullion, he was found to shine but the brighter and clearer the harder the attrition, while the glitter and tinsel of some of his more wordy contemporaries perished with the occasion which called for them. The effects of many a wise measure, suggested and enforced by him, will be felt in the future history of his loved State long after his body will have mouldered into her kindred dust.

But the inception of the bold policy of "Straight-out" Democratic nominations, and of openly throwing down the gauntlet to Radicalism in South Carolina, was pre-eminently due to Colonel M.C. Butler and General M.W. Gary, both of Edgefield. These gallant spirits not only made the first move, as we have shown, but they fought it through to triumphant adoption; and this, too, under discouragements which would have appalled most men. It was on their motion that Hampton was first called to the front; then gracefully falling back into the ranks, they have done yeoman service, earnest and unremitting, till victory perched on the glorious banner.

All honor, then, to these sons of Old Carolina – true champions of her noble women – who even in her darkest day, "did not despair of the Republic"!

But why extend this list? These are mentioned because a grateful people have already marked their names for posterity, and our narrative would be incomplete, without some tribute, however humble, to their well-earned fame.

And now, our task is done! Contrasting the first with the last chapter, who does not exclaim, "What hath GOD wrought!" *Then,* a conquered territory ruled by her former slaves; *now,* revived, as by the breath of the Almighty, into a glorious commonwealth – the *same* old State, with a proud record of nearly one hundred years! To-day she proudly leans on that hero-patriot, her own offspring, who has so gloriously "fought the good fight."

She smiles upon all her battle-scarred sons, who proudly love her with all the devotion of "Auld Lang Syne."

And she clasps to her bosom her rejoicing daughters, who had watched around her couch of suffering with such undying faith, and had scornfully resented all intrusion on the part of her heartless oppressors.

To the world, she once more proudly holds forth her time-honored escutcheon – re-baptized with the blood of some of her bravest and best.

"Animis opibusque parati."
"Dum spiro, spero."

APPENDIX

To render this faint outline of Reconstruction in South Carolina more distinct, and to show more fully the facts, now clearly established, which have formed the basis of some important statements in the foregoing pages, it is the purpose of the author to cull freely from official investigations already published by legislative authority. A "Joint Investigating Committee on Public Frauds," was appointed by the Senate and House of Representatives, and their labors, protracted through many months in 1877-78, resulted in the compilation of a formidable "Legislative Document" of 937 pages, a parallel to which can only be imagined in the lost records of Sodom and Gomorrah. As life is too short for every one to read everything, the size of the volume will, doubtless, deter many who are desirous of information; and a condensed statement of the most important topics may be very acceptable to these, and its greatly diminished proportions may attract the attention of the general reader.

The Committee give, very clearly, the beginnings of these frauds, and the *facilis descensus* is strikingly illustrated under the first head of

Supplies

Here, the legitimate expenses for stationery, postage stamps, etc., would be some ten dollars for each member for the session. But these improvised statesmen needed other help; and, among the first, are found, for each member, one Webster's unabridged dictionary, one calendar inkstand ($25), one gold pen ($10), and the privilege of using the Western Union Telegraph at the expense of the State. (The various railroad companies had already granted them free passes, for purposes of their own). Even these comparatively moderate indulgences would swell these accounts out of all proportion, and it was desirable to cover them from the too eager gaze of the taxpayer. It became necessary, therefore, to manipulate the Committee on Contingent Accounts; and, where all were equally implicated, this was easily effected. After their report on some honest claims, would follow the ominous words, "and others," or, "sundries and others," which would cover any amount of fraud. The Clerks of both Houses testified that bills for refreshments for committee rooms, groceries, clocks, horses and carriages, dry goods, furniture of every description, and miscellaneous articles of merchandise, were freely passed in this way. The contest was, which member should appropriate the most to his individual benefit. No wonder that the Committee would find, in the Treasurer's office, vouchers to show that, in a single session, three hundred and fifty thousand dollars were expended under the head of "supplies, sundries, and incidental expenses." Before the war, the whole State Government did not cost four hundred thousand dollars, all told.

(Page 8). Of this $35,000, $125,000 was expended for "refreshments," including the finest wines, liquors and cigars. In fact, this Committee on Contingencies had one of the largest committee rooms fitted up as a first-class restaurant, open from 8 o'clock, A.M., till 2 o'clock, A.M. of the following day, Sundays included. To all members, whether Radicals or Democrats, these refreshments were as free as the air they breathed; and the wonder is, that $125,000 could satisfy these hungering and thirsting statesmen for a whole session, particularly as they had the privilege of inviting State officials, judges, editors, reporters, and citizens generally.

The next highest item under the head of "supplies" is "furniture," and the Committee report (page 14) that not less than $200,000 had been paid out in four years, on this account alone. Dealers in Columbia testified to furnishing every committee room in the State House, and in the city, besides forty bed-rooms, *every session.* It was thus shown that these articles were taken home, on adjournment, as perquisites of the members. These dealers estimate that all the furniture in the State House, and in all the public offices, would not exceed, at original cost, $17,715; thus leaving $182,285 in four years, or more than $45,000 per annum, unaccounted for. Was it to be wondered at, that members who received $6 per diem, could yet afford elegant furniture for their rooms, Brussels carpets for their floors, and to recline on oriental spring and sponge mattresses – and all these to be renewed each successive session?

To show how readily a taste for luxuries can be cultivated at the expense of principle, the committee give the following contract:

1869-'70. – $5 clocks, 40-cent spittoons, $4 benches, straw beds, $1 chairs, $4 pine tables, 25-cent hat-pegs, $8 desks, $10 office desks, 50-cent coat-hooks, $4 looking-glasses, $2 window-curtains, $5 cornices, clay pipes, cheap whiskey.

1871-'72. – $600 clocks, $8 cuspadors, $200 crimson plush sofas, sponge mattresses and oriental pillows, $60 crimson plush gothic chairs, $80 library tables, $30 hat-racks, $50 desks, $80 to $175 office desks, $100 wardrobes, $600 mirrors, $600 brocaded curtains, lambrequins, etc., $80 walnut and gilt cor-nices, finest Havana cigars, champagne. (Page 24).

Rents, jewelry and stationery are the remaining items under this head of "supplies," but we will spare the reader the sickening details, simply remarking that the rents would, each year, have more than bought the fee-simple of the property rented; that the jewelry was enough to have decked the wives of certain sable statesmen like her of "Bambury Cross," even if her rings and bells had been pure gold; and the $68,000 per session for stationery would have abundantly supplied all the un-recon-structed States, for more than a year, in those literary necessities.

A place on this Committee on Contingencies was eagerly sought after, as it was a very sure bonanza.

They required all the bills to be itemized, but not added up; as they had their own rule for "addition, division, and silence." To these items they would prefix figures, whether tens, hundreds, or thousands; the value of the figure, as well as the number of prefixes, depending on the exigencies of the occasion.

Public Printing

We come now to more gigantic frauds, requiring a more extended sphere, and covering government officials, their partisan press, and the party leaders all over the State, as well as both branches of the Legislature. For years, under the "State Printer" system, whenever any large appropriation was wanted, the margin was extended sufficiently to cover all bribes and gratifications necessary to secure the requisite majority. To show the colossal proportions into which this system of "bribery and gratifications" had expanded, the Committee report that $98,500 was paid to secure the passage of one printing bill, in one session. (Page 218).

Seeing the immense appropriations thus secured, in the fall of 1870, the "Carolina Printing Company" was organized, consisting of Governor R.K. Scott, Attorney-General D.H. Chamberlain, Comptroller-General J. L. Neagle, Treasurer Niles G. Parker, J.W. Denny, J.W. Morris, and L. Cass Carpenter. This company owned the *Daily Union* of Columbia, and the *Charleston Republican*. (Page 215).

Besides these officials, whose constitutional duty it was to guard the Treasury by mutual checks and countersignings, this powerful Ring embraced, on its unofficial list, the Clerks of both Houses, to take care of the "circle of friends" in their respective bodies. Afterwards, "all State officials, judges, lawyers, editors, reporters, lobbyists – male and female – white and black – all, from the highest to the lowest, manifested deep interest in the passage of the Printing Company bills, and were paid according to their services and influence. (Page 217).

As the results of all these financial contrivances, the Committee give the following astounding facts and figures, established by copies of vouchers, and the testimony of witnesses, most of whom were active participants in the frauds.

"The amount appropriated and paid during the eight years, from 1868 to 1876, including the publication of general laws, and claims for printing, was $1,326,586! This sum is about double the cost for public printing, from the establishment of the State Government up to 1868; including all the payments made, during the war, in Confederate money." (Page 214).

Again, they say, on the same page: "The appropriations for public printing, and amounts paid newspapers for publishing Acts, in 1872-'73, reached $450,000, or $171,750 more than the printing cost the State for twenty-five years – commencing in 1841-'42 and ending in 1865-'66; including $42,141.63 paid during the war, in 1864, and in Confederate currency, for one year's printing.

"This amount of $450,000, also, exceeds the cost of like work in Massachusetts, Pennsylvania, Ohio, Maryland, and New York, by $122,932.13; embracing, as they do, five of the largest and most populous of the Northern, Eastern, Southern and Western States."

In 1873-'74, another stunning appropriation of $385,000 was made, making $835,000 in fifteen months, or an average of $145,594 over and above the cost of printing in all the Southern States for the year 1878. (Page 215).

In one of the "exhibits" of the Committee stands; this telling contrast:

Cost of printing per month, under Radical rule . . $55,666.00
Cost of printing per month, under Hampton rule . . . $514.80

The Committee, in receiving returns from the several States, as to the printing expenses of these eight years, were somewhat startled at the following official report from Louisiana, her nearest of kin in affliction:

In 1868, paid for printing $125,343.00
In 1869, paid for printing 439,345.00
In 1870, paid for printing 317,135.00
In 1871, paid for printing 362,493.00
In 1872, paid for printing 154,752.00
In 1873, paid for printing 172,891.00
In 1874, paid for printing 158,801.00
In 1875, paid for printing 200,000.00
In 1876, paid for printing 148,816.92
In 1877, paid for printing 40,528.71

$2,120,105.63

Very respectfully, etc.,

Louis Leonard,

Chairman Committee on Printing.

This gives an excess of Louisiana printing bills over those of South Carolina of $793,519.63, just about the difference in resources of the two States, under the equally skillful and unscrupulous manipulation of *their* carpet-bag gentry.

We will close this very general analysis of these stupendous frauds in the words of the Committee:

"The history of the Carolina Printing Company, the "Republican Printing Company," and their offshoots, the *Columbia Daily Union*, and the *Charleston Republican* (if the testimony is to be believed, and, surely, who can doubt its truth, corroborated, as it is, in all essential particulars?) is sufficient, in any court, to consign almost every person connected with them to the penitentiary for life. Some of the parties to these great crimes are now in prison; whilst many others, having deserted their luxurious homes and fire-sides, are fugitives from justice, skulking abroad. They and all connected with them in these atrocious deeds should feel deeply grateful that the people of South Carolina, governed by wise and prudent counsels, have attempted and will only attempt to bring them to punishment by due process of law, instead of rising up long ago, in a storm of just indignation and wrath, and sweeping them from the face of the earth.

"Perhaps a vail of charity should, in some degree, be

thrown over the poor and ignorant colored men who have been deceived, misled, and incriminated by artful, corrupt and shameless leaders; but if, in the exercise of great generosity and forbearance; these poor and ignorant men shall be spared, it should teach them none the less, that dishonesty and fraud will eventually meet a merited punishment." (Page 252).

To scramble out of this filthy, Serbonian bog and plunge into another equally deep, and, probably, more extensive, we must hold our breath and noses, and venture into the confines, at least, of the

Pay Certificates

This, too, sprung from small beginnings. The Speaker of the House, and the President of the Senate, being authorized to sign these for their respective Houses, the temptation to multiply soon became irresistible, as they were supreme in this department. The committee soon reached such facts as this:

"The House actually employed eight laborers, and from five to ten pages. Yet we have certificates from the Treasurer's office, showing that as many as 159 laborers, and 124 pages were paid during one session; and for many sessions. Certificates were issued for fifty pages, many of whom were children of members." (Page 398).

But such results as these soon dwindled into mere pin-money, when contrasted with what followed in an astonishingly short time.

The committee say, "To perpetuate the power and influence of the Radical party, it was necessary to have a ready and unfailing reservoir of funds; and no simpler or easier way suggested itself than these certificates. Thus it became not only possible, but practicable to perpetuate the numerous frauds in the public printing and supplies to which we have already alluded. Indeed, this, like the famous Hydra, threw out its hundred heads, encircling and poisoning every department of the government, and giving comfort and support to local leaders. This immense fund produced and nurtured a Bond-Ring, a Printing-Ring, and this Legislative-Ring – the most popular, and, at the same time, the most unscrupulous. It is evident, from the testimony, that such a fund as this was necessary to silence any complaint within their own ranks, and to pacify the fears of the timid, and the greed of the avaricious, while the other great Rings were in successful progress." (Page 389.) While the Bond-Ring composed of a limited number of State officers were revelling in their mammoth speculations in bonds, with Kimpton, as their unfailing bank; this Legislative-Ring could only successfully contend with them, for their share of the taxes, through this certificate-contrivance, manipulated by Solomon's swindling depository for State taxes, called by the imposing name of the "Carolina Loan and Trust Co." Of this institution the Committee say, "It is now known that the bank referred to (Solomon's), was inaugurated in fraud, supported by a ring of political pirates, composed of Chamberlain, Scott, Parker and other officials, and exhibited, during its existence, a series of corruptions and robberies unknown in the history of any other corporation." (Page 525).

These certificates soon reached magnificent proportions, ranging from $500, to $5,000 on a single paper. For these larger ones, a conference was generally called of the presiding officers of both Houses, the State Treasurer, and the chairmen of the Finance Committees of both Houses. Of course, the State was entirely powerless against a conspiracy of her own guardians; and we are not astounded when the committee say, "The table submitted with this report, shows, among other things, that in *one session* there was issued $1,168,255, in pay certificates (not including printing certificates), every dollar of which was a robbery, with the exception of about $200,000, due members and legally appointed attachees of the General Assembly." (Page 390).

Sometimes there was a co-operation between the "Bond" and "Certificate" powers, and then the Treasury would collapse. This was notably the case when "A Joint Special Investigating Committee," familiarly called in the parlance of that day, "The High Old Joint," was appointed in 1871-'72, to examine the books of the Financial Agent, Kimpton, with reference mainly to the Sinking Fund. The appointment of this committee was merely "a tub to the whale," in answer to the tax-payers. It consisted of B. F. Whittemore and S. A. Swails, of the Senate, and Jno. B. Dennis, Wm. H. Gardner, and Tim. Hurley, of the House – five of the head devils in all financial rascality. Kimpton was in New York City, and it was necessary to go there for the investigation. In fact, another grand conspiracy was going on in New York, requiring the presence there, not only of Kimpton, but of Governor Scott, Treasurer Parker, and Secretary of State Cardozo. The last named having taken the Great Seal of the State along with him. This conspiracy was, then and there to sign, seal, and put on the market, without any semblance of authority, six millions of the "Sterling Bonds." This grand scheme was frustrated, after the bonds had been executed, and just before they would have been put upon the market, by an accidental discovery of the fraud through a clerk in the "American Bank-Note Company." (Page 425).

But to return to our "High Old Joint." They at once became more concerned about their pay than their duties, and as there was much doubt as to the proper fund on which they could draw, they consulted Attorney-General Chamberlain, who was always fertile in expedients. His advice was to look directly to Kimpton, who would pay out handsomely. After making some preliminary drafts on the "Armed Force Fund," and others, they went on leisurely, to Kimpton's quarters in New York, where they found Chamberlain awaiting them. The matter of expenses was soon satisfactorily arranged, and as Kimpton complained of having been overworked recently, and of needing rest, a recess of one month was cheerfully granted him, during which Whittemore went to his old home in Massachusetts, Swails went to Elmira, N. Y., Dennis to New Haven, Hurley to Boston, and Gardner accompanied Kimpton to Saratoga. Kimpton wanted this margin of time to "cook the books" of his agency, and make them ready for the inspection of this virtuous Committee, not from any fear of exposure, but to deprive the members of the opportunity and pretext of blackmail. (Page 393.)

He paid their expenses liberally, $3,108 being the largest, and $1,284 the smallest sum paid any single member of the Committee. The Chairman estimated the advances thus made at $12,501.32, and yet Kimpton charged the State the even $17,000, under this head, and every dollar of this amount was included in Kimpton's account against the State, and balanced in the settlement made with him by Scott, Parker and Chamberlain, when they left their offices in 1872. (Page 293.)

Frank Moses was impatient at remaining at home, when such luxurious pickings were to be enjoyed in New York, so he had himself summoned to give information on the purchase of arms, under his administration, as Adjutant-General. On his return he made out, as Speaker, a pay certificate in favor of some fictitious name, for $2,500. He had no difficulty in procuring the signature of the Chairman of the "High Old Joint," but, as a Joint Committee, it required the signature of the President of the Senate. The virtuous Lieutenant-Governor, Ransier, positively refused his official signature until the amount was raised to $5,000, and he permitted to share and share alike with the Speaker. (Page 394.)

Another item of expense was the precise sum of $3,887.44 to the Printing Company for stationery furnished the same Committee!

Several pay certificates in favor of "experts" – when it was in evidence that *not one* expert had been employed – threw a sum of about $3,000 into the capacious pockets of Whittemore. (Page 427.)

Besides the liberal allowance paid by Kimpton, other members, either by direct charges for services rendered, or by fraudulent certificates like those of Whittemore, drew some $12,000 directly from the State.

Summing up all the vouchers of whatever kind, it was found that the pay of these "investigators" varied from $60 per day for the highest, and $20 for the lowest, for ninety-two days. (Page 393).

By way of contrasting the resources of Radicals and Democrats at this time, take the following: The tax-payers, goaded almost to frenzy at the ruinous tax bills levied, and the corruption and robbery now as evident as the noon-day sun, and as unblushing, too, called a convention to send a commission to Washington to lay the facts of the case before the national administration. With some difficulty a contribution of some eight hundred dollars was raised from an impoverished people to pay the expenses of this mission.

The Radicals, on the other hand, had only to wink at a pay certificate in favor of "F. L. Christopher" (F. L. Cardoza, at that time treasurer), for $2500, and soon *their* Committee, with Whittemore at its head, and Cardozo himself at its tail, were wending their way to Washington, to forestall this desperate effort of despairing men. Thus the tax-payers were forced, in addition to their own contributions, to pay, at the rate of three to one, the expenses of the thieves themselves sent on to thwart all their appeals! It is needless to say which Committee was successful. (Page 390).

These emboldened thieves did not always wait for some great occasion to rob the treasury, but very many instances are recorded where two or more would play at the game successfully. In 1871-'72, J. J. Patterson proposed to Speaker Moses to turn over to him blank pay certificates, which he (Patterson) would have filled up in favor of fictitious parties to the amount of $30,000; for which he would advance to Moses $10,000 in cash. This contract was promptly carried out, and the cash checks in favor of Moses, one for $7,000, and the other for $3,000, were in evidence before the Committee, as also were the fictitious pay-certificates, all in the handwriting of one Jacobs, cashier of "Solomon's Bank." (Page 399).

On another occasion, Cardozo, as treasurer, found an unexpended balance of $75,000 appropriation, remaining in the treasury to the amount of $4,000. This anomaly he determined to turn to his own benefit. He wanted the signatures of the presiding officers and Clerks of both Houses, and, as usual, took them in as partners in the fraud. Abundant evidence was before the Committee of pay certificates, of $800 each, in favor of Gleaves, Lieutenant-Governor; S.J. Lee, Speaker; Woodruff Clerk of the Senate; and Jones, Clerk of the House; and Cardozo, Treasurer. The name assumed by Cardozo in this transaction was "C. L. Frankfort." On this he has been indicted, and tried by a jury mostly of his race and party, and found "guilty." (Page 372).

Sometimes these certificates, in small amounts, were freely given parties who could tell or invent tales of Ku-Kluxism, or of any other suffering on account of party. (Page 390).

The evidence also shows that visiting strangers, often from other States, would receive complimentary legislative certificates before leaving. (Page 400).

And how does all this deviltry sum up? The committee show, by an "Exhibit," that this account of "legislative expenses" averaged $585,369.29, *annually*, from 1870 to 1874, exclusive of printing; while under Governor Hampton's administration of 1876-'77, under very adverse circumstances, the same account reached $77,119, *printing included.* (Page 407). The whole amount of appropriations for these four sessions was $1,085,000, *less the printing;* whilst the actual expenditures reached $2,341,461.16! (Page 407).

Could a few intelligent scoundrels, with both houses filled with lunatics, have accomplished more amazing feats of rascality?

The remainder of the report under this head trenches upon those interminable bond-issues – a bottomless pit which can never be fully investigated but by the light of eternity. As far as known, any clear statement would require a book of itself, and then the unexplored would seem as broad and dark as when we began.

Through Chamberlain's influence, Hiram H. Kimpton, an old college comrade of his, had been appointed financial agent of the State. All these bonds were manipulated by him. The only tribunal to which he was responsible, was the "Board of Finance," for four years, consisting of Scott, Chamberlain and Parker. Stupendous frauds were perpetrated under this organization, and never a murmur of dissent was heard from any individual member. These facts require no comment. In the

Greenville and Columbia Railroad Swindle

we will attempt some short analysis of the frauds so fully brought to light. J.J. Patterson now comes to the front, and his pre-eminent financial skill in all railroad swindles landed him finally in Congress, where he has served full six years as U.S. Senator.

His first achievement was in carrying through the Legislature a contract for rebuilding the Blue Ridge Railroad, which he afterwards caused to be annulled, for the benefit of the State, by the snug little sum of eighty thousand dollars, to him, in hand, paid. (Page 563).

He then turned his eyes to the Greenville and Columbia Railroad, and organized a company of twelve, embracing all the State officials, with Kimpton at the head, and, to do the dirtiest of their work in the house, Joe Crews was taken as the tail. Each share was valued at $20,000, but Patterson's genius was shown in getting up this quarter of a million in stock without any party being called on for a quarter of a cent.

The State owned 21,698 shares in the road, at $20 per share, aggregating $433,960. Besides this, she held a lien for indemnity for the million and a half in bonds guaranteed by her solemn act.

To reach a sale of the shares, Patterson procured an Act to be passed creating a Sinking Fund Commission, and authorizing them to sell all unproductive property belonging to the State. Ostensibly, the object of this act was to authorize the sale of damaged marble, granite, &c., lying about the State House grounds, but the terms of the act were elastic enough to cover all her railroad and real estate property. The very day after its passage, the shares of the Greenville and Columbia Railroad were sold to the above mentioned company, at the nominal price of $2.75 per share, without any advertisement, and without any money being paid. How this was managed can be *guessed* from these facts: that Scott, Chamberlain and Neagle formed the majority of the sinking lurid commission, and were also stockholders in this new company of twelve; and that the cherubic Kimpton, the officer to invest the proceeds of sale, held two shares in the same company. (Page 563).

But this did not give them a majority of the stock, and it became necessary to buy up enough from private shareholders. Selecting two natives, with empty purses and elastic consciences, for $10,000 each, they easily procured their names and influence for the purchase of a sufficient number of shares, at $2.75, to give them the unquestionable control of the road. They soon devised a scheme for the transfer of all the State shares to themselves, and the purchase money for private stockholders was furnished by Kimpton. (Page 564.)

As to the million and a half lien on the road, held by the State, another Act was hurried through the Legislature by bribery, and under its forced provisions the lien was postponed to bonds, to be issued under a second mortgage; thus enabling the ring to divide and put their bonds on the market, while the only security held by the State was swept away, and a contingent debt of fifteen hundred thousand dollars fixed upon the State, without indemnity. Thus, in the words of the Committee, "this ring secured to themselves comparatively miserable morsels of plunder, whilst the State was robbed of millions to carry out the scheme." (Page 565.)

How Kimpton managed to furnish so much cash is easily accounted for. The Financial Board bought the authority, by Act of the Legislature, to settle with the Financial Agent. Kimpton's report of the sale of over $8,000,000 of bonds was before the Committee, and for nine-tenths of this enormous amount there is no mention made of any rates of sale. There were only four items of sales in the report, and two of them were, respectively, $2,843,000 bonds sold on one day, and $4,214,500 sold on another. Of course he had it in his power to make as great a difference between the rates of the actual and reported sales as he chose, and the Financial Board actually settled with him on the basis of this report. (Page 567.)

With this convenient arrangement there was no limit to their liberality in bribing. Moses was Speaker, and feeling his importance in their Legislative schemes, he fixed a high price on his connivance. Kimpton agreed to give him $25,000 for the privilege of appointing certain Committees of the House. But as $113,000 of this amount was already covered by a mortgage held by Kimpton on him, personally, he was indifferent about recognizing the appropriate persons in debate. One important measure was about to be postponed by dilatory motions, made by parties who thought they had not received as much as they were worth, and Moses rather aided their schemes. Patterson, as lobbyist, seeing the danger, sent Dennis to Moses' chair, with the instruction, "Go and ask that damned scoundrel how much he wants." The answer came back promptly, "$10,000 over and above every thing." "Tell him, all right; he shall have it." But Moses was still "dilatory," till the promise was reduced to writing and put into the hands of his confidential friend, Joe Crews. (Page 511.)

The Impeachment Swindle

These bond-frauds were so gross and palpable that, in December, 1871, C. C. Bowen, one of the disaffected, actually introduced into the Legislature a resolution of impeachment against R. K. Scott, as representing the Board of Finance. Knowing Kimpton's resources, and the venality of the tribunal, Chamberlain was as calm as a summer's eve. Not so with Scott and Parker; and their evident alarm only afforded another opportunity for the display of Patterson's genius, in finding "good stealing," even in this side-issue. By his henchman, Worthington, he gave encouragement to the measure by day, and by night he personally worked on the fears of Scott and Parker; thus "running with the hare, and holding with the hounds." When he had fully succeeded, and Scott and Parker were helplessly alarmed, he proposed a panacea which Worthington and himself alone could administer. That was the notorious warrants on the Armed Force Fund – one for "Mooney," of $25,000; a second for Legget, of $10,600; and a third for "David H. Wilson," of $13,000. Of course no such persons had ever lived, to their knowledge. With this snug little $49,100, he promised to make all lovely for him in the Legislature, and fulfilled his promise with probably a tithe of the amount. (Page 583).

The report on this mere by-play gives some very interesting reading, but, compared with his mammoth jobs of rascality in that day, was only an interlude for Patterson. But his peculiar genius for swindling found full play in the passage of the Acts called, respectively,

The Blue Ridge Railroad Scrip, the Validating Act, and the Financial Settlement.

Having bought the position of President of the Blue Ridge Railroad, he soon afterwards announced a grand scheme to relieve the State of her $4,000,000 guaranty on its bonds, by the issue of "scrip," ostensibly to pay all the honest debts of the Blue Ridge Railroad Company; but, in fact, to be converted into a private and personal fund, for purposes of corruption. By a system of wholesale bribery – the details of which were furnished the Committee, mainly, by the parties bribed – his bill soon became a law. This elevated him to a platform of rascality as high as Kimpton himself; and we soon find him dictating the terms to Kimpton on which he would furnish the means for purchasing votes enough to secure the passage of the iniquitous "Validating" and "Financial Settlement" Acts. Here is the precious document in full, the original having been furnished the Committee by Treasurer Parker himself:

Vice-President's Office
Greenville & Columbia R. R. Co.
Columbia, S. C., March 4, 1872.

Hon. Niles G. Parker,
State Treasurer, South Carolina:

Please deliver to H. H. Kimpton, "revenue bond scrip," due the Blue Ridge Railroad Company, according to

Act passed March 2, 1872, amounting to one hundred and
fourteen thousand two hundred and fifty dollars, at par,
upon the following conditions: That forty-two thousand
eight hundred and fifty-seven dollars of said scrip, at par, is
to be used for paying the expenses of passing through the
House of Representatives bills styled, "A Bill relating to the
bonds of the State of South Carolina," and "A Bill to authorize the Financial Board to settle the accounts of the Financial Agent." Now, if these above named bills are passed and
become laws, this order for forty-two thousand eight hundred and fifty-seven dollars, in scrip, at par, is to be paid
said Kimpton; and, if not passed, then this order for that
amount to be void, and the scrip is not to be delivered. Also,
that seventy-one thousand four hundred and fourteen dollars
of scrip, at par, you shall deliver to said Kimpton, if said
bills become laws, and provided he shall pay the sum of
fifty thousand dollars, the proceeds of said scrip at seventy
cents on the dollar, in paying the expenses already incurred,
in passing through the Senate the bill known as "A Bill to
relieve the State of all liability on account of guaranty of
Blue Ridge Railroad bonds, etc.," passed March 2, 1872,
which said expenses said Kimpton has contracted to pay;
and if the said Kimpton fails or refuses to pay said amounts
in defraying said expenses (when required by me), then this
order to be void. If said conditions are complied with, and
the amount of said scrip delivered to Kimpton, he is not to
be held liable for, or to account for its value. The above two
sums of $42,859 and $71,414, in scrip, at par, make up the
amount of scrip first mentioned in this order.

John J. Patterson,
President of Blue Ridge Railroad Co. in S. C.

Witness: R. B. Elliott.

In the language of the Committee, "comment, criticism,
or denunciation would only weaken the force of such a document." (Page 614).

Of the two Acts above mentioned, the first appeared to be
merely an Act to validate the irregular issue of certain bonds; but
was really intended to legalize the illegal use and disposition of

$6,000,000 of State bonds by Kimpton, and then to fasten such debt upon the State.

The second, simply empowered the notorious Financial Board to make a settlement with Kimpton, as Financial Agent; but really afforded the desired opportunity of covering up and cancelling the large amounts paid out by Kimpton, from sales of bonds illegally made, to be divided out among the Ring as "commissions," and in carrying the purchase of the Greenville and Columbia Railroad by the same ring.

All these measures were passed, of course; but the Blue Ridge scrip came to grief; Patterson and Scott were not in the same boat in this matter, and it did not suit the Governor to have the great bulk of the next year's taxes collected in Patterson's scrip. He, therefore, had the Treasurer of Richland enjoined from receiving them for taxes; and the case, going up to the Supreme Court, was finally decided against this scrip as State legal tender. There was evidence before the Committee that Patterson attempted to bribe this tribunal also, but his money did not go farther than the bottomless pit of Frank Moses' purse.

The next Legislature passed an Act repealing Patterson's Blue Ridge swindle, but his timely bribe of $1,000 caused the Chairman of the Engrossing Committee to *lose* it between the Senate Chamber and the Executive office, where it should have gone, for the Governor's signature. This gave Patterson one year more to secure his pilferings. (Page 646).

Dropping Patterson for a time, we must permit D. H. Chamberlain to come to the front, out of that professional bomb-proof, where he had, all along, so securely ensconced himself. In the matter of

The Ku-Klux Rewards,

he figured largely as "attorney in fact" for Brevet-Colonel Lewis Merrill, U. S. A. In 1871, Governor Scott had issued a proclamation offering a reward of $200 for each person arrested, with proof to convict of the charge, under the "Enforcement," commonly known as the "Ku-Klux Act."

Some allusions have already been made, in this book, to the persecutions in York County, under the indefatigable and unscrupulous administration of Lewis Merrill, Brevet-Colonel, U. S. A. We now find the true stimulus to his patriotic zeal and great ardor in the discharge of his high military trusts, when the time for "rewards" had come.

The lavish waste of the public money, under the head of these rewards, began with one Hester, a "reformed Ku-Klux," under whose single evidence so many poor creatures had been sent to the penitentiary. Hester demanded $18,600 under the Governor's proclamation, for ninety-three arrests and convictions. This little bill rather staggered Scott, and he was disposed to put him off under the plea of "no funds." The next day, Hester returned with a recommendation from Chamberlain, as Attorney-General, that the amount be paid from the "Armed Force Fund," which was carried out to the mutual satisfaction of client and attorney. (Page 653).

During the Session of 1871-'72, an Act was passed appropriating the sum of $35,000 to pay the claims under this proclamation. It was in evidence before the Committee, that both Attorney-General Chamberlain and Major Merrill were very active and urgent in lobbying this Act through the Legislature. It was finally passed – the rewards to be paid by the Governor. Moses being the chief executive, this did not suit the parties mainly interested. So, he was "induced" to turn the matter of the disbursement over to a commission of five – of which commission, D. H. Chamberlain was chairman. The vouchers show warrants in favor of Merrill to the amount of $15,750, and an additional order on the Armed Force Fund for $500 to re-imburse the United States Government for money advanced in this army hunt after the Ku-Klux.

There was another award of $1,200 to one Byron, Private Secretary to Governor Moses, and confidential adviser to Merrill. The Committee call particular attention to the course of Chamberlain, as follows:

"Whilst he was Attorney-General of the State, recommending officially to the Governor, the payment of this large claim to Hester, based upon his assumed arrest of ninety-three persons, under the proclamation, the payment to be made out of the Armed Force Fund, which he knew to be illegal.

"Afterwards, as a lobby agent, using his influence to have the appropriation of $35,000 passed. As the attorney in fact of Merrill, persuading Governor Moses to appoint a commission to do, what the Act required the Governor himself to do; procuring himself to be appointed chairman of the commission for the distribution of said fund; and, whilst so deeply interested, presiding, hearing, and joining in the decision of this matter; and, after the awards were made, collecting and receiving the amount of Merrill's warrants, indorsing them 'D. H. Chamberlain, attorney in fact for Lewis Merrill;' and, with his associates, appropriating $500 each out of the money appropriated by law to pay rewards, under a proclamation of Governor Scott.

"The conflict of interests represented by him is plain enough. How he was able to do exact and impartial justice to his client and the State, is not so clear. The bald fact stands out, that his client, Maj. Lewis Merrill, U. S. A., with his $15,750 'rewards,' was well taken care of." (Page 655.)

Of Lewis Merrill, Brevet-Colonel, United States Army, they say:

"The testimony shows that he (Merrill) made himself unusually active and officious in procuring the passage of the appropriation of $35,000 through the Legislature. He enlisted the services of the private secretary of the Governor in his interests, and was himself rewarded with the lion's share – a result not to be surprised at, when he had Attorney-General Chamberlain, Chairman of the Commission, in his employ. During all these arduous labors, this creature Merrill was in the receipt of his usual pay and commutation as a field officer in the army of the United States." (Page 655.)

The Committee obtained from the records of the United States Circuit Court a certificate, under seal, from the clerk, that one hundred and nine cases gave the sum total of all who had been convicted, or pleaded guilty, under these Ku-Klux indictments, which would call for $21,800 under the proclamation; and yet every dollar of the $35,000 was expended.

The only point where Patterson showed his paw, was in having his tool, Worthington, appointed assistant counsel in the prosecutions, at the moderate compensation of $3,500 per annum. He himself was after larger game.

The gratification, entertainment and amusement offered the new-fledged voters in enrolling the whole

Militia

of the State, exclusively of colored troops, turned out very expensive under the administration of the spendthrift Moses as Adjutant-General. The Committee say that "just previous to the general election in 1870, more than $100,000 was expended; and, indeed, the simple enrollment absorbed over $200,000 of the public funds. This money furnished favorites with individual campaign funds, to be used in securing their election to the Legislature, or county offices; and those favored persons, in their turn, were expected to operate as auxiliaries to perpetuate the power of the party and of the ring." (Page 667).

The Moses contracts for furnishing arms to these sable warriors are too disgusting even for association with the foregoing black catalogue.

By way of episode, we insert one or two specimens from the Committee's vouchers, mainly to confirm certain statements in our accounts of the Laurens troubles. On page 675 will be found this explicit document:

Laurens, S. C., July 8, 1870.

"Capt. Hubbard,
            Chief Constable.

Dear Sir: Your letter of the 2d was received to-day, enclosing the money due me. It came in good time. We are going to have a hard campaign up here, and we must have more constables. *I will carry the election here with the militia, if the constables will work with me.* I am giving out ammunition all the time. Tell Scott he is all right here now. Let me know how times are below.

Respectfully,
Joseph Crews."

Also, on pages 683 and 684, the following receipts as Lieutenant-Colonel and Aid to the Governor:

"Received this 13th day of June, 1870, of General Dennis, Acting Ordnance Officer, the following:

13th June, 1870-300 rifle muskets, 300 bayonet-scabbards, 300 tompions, 300 screw-drivers and wrenches, 25 tumbler punches, 300 cartridge boxes, 300 cap pouches, 300 waist belts and plates, 300 gun slings, 12 arm chests, 2000 rounds of ammunition.

2nd August, 1870-320 rifle muskets, 320 bayonets and scabbards, 320 tompions, 320 screw-drivers and wrenches, 80 tumbler punches, 320 cartridge boxes, 320 cartridge box belts, 320 cap pouches, 320 waist belts and plates, 320 gun slings, 12 arm chests, 8,000 rounds of ammunition (!).

Joseph Crews,
Lieutenant-Colonel and A. D. C."

Finally, this other, which "followed hard upon": (Page 685.)

"Received at Columbia, this 25th day of September, 1870, ten thousand rounds of ammunition, (Rem. Pat.)

Y. J. P. Owens."

The Armed Force Fund

authorized to be drawn from any funds in the treasury, not otherwise appropriated, was even more abused than the militia fund, as we have seen from the preceding pages. Of the Armed Force, or "Constabulary," as it was more familiarly called, the Committee say:

"All through the testimony it will be seen that this 'Force' was used, not to preserve the peace, but to carry elections for the party, and to intimidate those not of the party. One hundred and fifty-one deputy constables were appointed, on full per diem and mileage, and over five hundred to do special service, just before and during elections. Many were mounted, armed and equipped to do service and scour the country from county to county; and to perform the peculiar services alluded to in their daily and weekly reports to the chief constable, (Hubbard.) This bosom friend and confidential adviser of the Governor consolidated all these reports for his information, on such points as how many political meetings they had attended, political condition of county or township, and how many of them could be elected to the Legislature or county offices. A large number of these deputies had been imported from Ohio *and* Pennsylvania – friends of Scott and Patterson – and it is interesting to know that more than twenty of them succeeded in obtaining seats in the Legislature." (Page 702.)

There was one instance; in this importation of "bummers," when Scott was well nigh "hoist by his own petard."

Union County was considered very doubtful in the then coming election. The ordinary means of intimidation, through the constabulary, having failed in that community, Scott sent one C. C. Baker on to New York City, to bring on thirty-two of the hardest cases he could find, under pretext of working a gold mine in that county, but, in fact, to overawe and harass.

These were in addition to the 151 above mentioned, and were to be specially armed with Winchester rifles and navy pistols. Hubbard testified before the Committee in these words: "I don't think it would have been possible to have selected, or even to have found a more dangerous lot of men in any city in the Union." Certainly, if *L. B. Hubbard* says this, they must have approximated devils incarnate very nearly.

Hubbard goes on: "As Scott could not comply with all their demands, he became much demoralized and frightened, fearing they would kill *him*. At his request, I paid them all off liberally, bought through tickets for them from Columbia to New York, via Charleston steamer, and saw them all safely embarked. He was afraid lest any *one* of them should be left in Columbia."

The constituted authorities of New York may thus take comfort from the fact that the purlieus of their city did furnish a body of men who could "demoralize" and "frighten" the head devil of Radicalism in South Carolina at his own game.

The Penitentiary

was an unceasing drain on the Treasury for ten long years, the greater part of which flowed into the private purses of superintendents, directors, and Hardy Solomon, of course.

South Carolina had no penitentiary before the war, but in the violent changes in our institutions after the war, it was one of the first acts of Orr's administration (1866) to establish one. Major Thos. B. Lee, a very skillful engineer and architect, and a man of the highest integrity, was selected as the first Superintendent. Of him the Committee say: "The whole expenditure passed, and deficiencies due from 1866 to 1877 exceed $900,000, of which the two years' term of Major Lee is chargeable with about one-sixth – which, contrasted with the work since done, and the amount expended, gives the highest evidence of his faithfulness, economy, and fitness for the office, and fully vindicates the good judgment of Governor Orr's appointment." (Page 773). Major Lee's term was for more than two years, during which the main buildings were erected, and the expensive machinery for self-sustaining labor was introduced.

But Scott saw too much money flowing that way, from the Treasury, to suffer it to go into honest hands, and he soon trumped up trivial causes for the removal of Lee. When he gave Stolbrand – one of his own kidney and people – the place, he began to feel comfortable. His first operation was to loan Stolbrand, as Superintendent, $15,000 on a deposit of $30,000 in warrants on the Treasury, and then quietly to ignore the loan and collect the collaterals. Stolbrand himself, in conniving with the directors on the one hand, and Hardy Solomon on the other, made money so fast, that the place was adjudged worthy of higher financial talents, and more finished rascality, so he had to "step down and out;" and General Dennis, one of the carpet-bag princes, reigned in his stead. His directors were Neagle, Comptroller-General; W. B. Nash, colored Senator from Richland, and Hayne, colored Secretary of State. And now the system of stealing was somewhat simplified, by having Dennis, Nash, and Hayne as the inner ring, and Dennis, Neagle, and Solomon as the outer ring. Nash had a brickyard, and his bills for bricks furnished would go far to throw a Chinese wall around the whole of Columbia; while Hayne, with no wood yard at all, furnished fuel enough to burn all of Nash's bricks. These accounts had to be audited by the outer ring, who were all the while playing that game with the Treasury which the boys used to call "heads I win, tails you lose."

In addition to his peculiar *assistance,* through his bank, Solomon furnished the convicts with all their edible supplies; and the single article of "bacon" would allow a ration of seven pounds to each per day. But what shall we say when we see items, and large ones, too, for brandy, whiskey, cigars, sardines, citrons, raisins, chocolate, almonds, etc., etc.? (Page 775).

But we will dismiss this subject with the single remark, that the Committee have published evidence enough, established by official vouchers, too, to put into this institution for life all who were officially connected with it, under either Stolbrand or Dennis.

Even the institutions of charity, such as

The Colored Orphan Asylum,
and the Transient Sick and Poor,

eventually fell under the management of unscrupulous thieves, thus verifying, and making literally true, the figurative language used by the Committee almost at the beginning of their report, when they say that "the frauds, perjuries, embezzlements and larceny of the party in power, covered every transaction and article, from the cradle of the infant to the coffin and cerements of the dead."

Of the former, we will only say that their bills of supply would do credit to a first class restaurant in a large city; and their dry goods, millinery, and almost every article of female attire, would be appropriate only to the most extravagant female colleges.

"The transient sick and poor of the various towns and cities of this State" reached down to the coffin and the undertaker. The largest voucher under this head was a draft in favor of that eminent philanthropist, Hardy Solomon, for $2,500. The orders were comparatively small, and many of them in favor of political tramps passing through Columbia. Notably was one in favor of Col. Kirk – he of "Kirk's Lambs" in North Carolina – to help him on his way from Augusta to Washington City.

Our task is almost done. If it wearies and disgusts the reader merely to examine these specimen sheets, how must it be with him who has to delve in all this mire and filth to give posterity some insight into the pandemonium to which a sovereign State of this Union has been subjected, helplessly, for eight long years?

We *must,* however, refer the reader to the report itself for details – if he can stand them – under the more personal headings of

Loan to F.J. Moses, Governor's Contingent Fund,
Hardy Solomon's Claim, Treasurer's Due Bills,
Election of T.C. Dunn, Bribery by Chamberlain in
Whaley's Case, Dunn and the Life Insurance,
W.J. Whipper and His Certificates.

The last mentioned, name (Whipper) figures largely in this report, though we have passed him over, so far, unnoticed. He was the colored representative from Beaufort, and elected Circuit Judge with F. J. Moses, though neither of them were permitted to disgrace the Bench. There is one voucher in his case which we will insert mainly to show the estimate he placed on his own professional ability. (Page 853.)

W. Whipper, in account with Sinking Fund,
State of South Carolina.

1872	Dr.	
January	To amount received from the City of Charleston per sale of Powder Magazine, one-third of $7,100	$2,368.00
"	To amount received from H. Bischoff, for lot of land on Line and Meeting street, Charleston, one-third of $6,875 .	2,291.66
"	To amount received from J.S. Riggs, for lot of land on Line street, one-third of $550	183.33
March	To amount received from A. McBee, for State works and grounds, Greenville, one-third of $2,850	950.00
"	To amount received from Pleasant Barton, first instalment of lease of State-road, Greenville	725.00
		$6,517.99
January	By auctioneer's commission on $7,100, at 2½ per ct	$177.50
"	By auctioneer's commission on $876, at 2½ per ct .	171.87
"	By auctioneer's commission on $550, at 2½ per ct .	13.75

March	By auctioneer's commission on sale of State works and State-road, and papers, stamps and expenses	$206.37
"	By cash paid for advertising, *Charleston Courier* . .	242.75
"	By cash paid for advertising, *Daily News*	247.05
"	By cash paid for advertising, *Beaufort Times*	32.00
"	By cash paid for advertising, *Beaufort Republican* . . .	32.00
"	By amount due W. J. Whipper as attorney	7,033.33
		$8,156.62

Recapitulation.

Debtor by receipts	$6,517.99
Creditor by payments	8,156.62
Due W. J. W.	$1,638.63

Now, J. L. Neagle, Comptroller-General, and associate with Scott and Chamberlain, as "Sinking Fund Commission," on page 854, testifies that Whipper, as Secretary of the Commission, was authorized to sell some real estate in Charleston, *but was never employed as attorney.*

In the same evidence before the Committee, Neagle gave the particulars of the sale of all the stock held by the State in the Greenville and Columbia Railroad, in the South Carolina Railroad and Southwestern Railroad Bank, in the Cheraw and Coalfield Railroad, and in the Blue Ridge Railroad. The last item was $1,320,000, at one dollar per share.

All the unused real estate to which the State held titles,

both in Columbia and Charleston, was also sold, and all this, railroads and real estate, under an Act purporting to cover the sale of some perishable rubbish in and about the State House grounds.

The final chapter in this book of frauds, is exclusively devoted to the monstrous and unblushing bribery and corruption in the case of

John J. Patterson and the United States Senate.

The committee give sixty-five pages of testimony, wherein is clearly set forth the testimony of seventy-five witnesses given under a promise of immunity as "State's evidence." Most of these were members of the Legislature, who received, in hand paid, the bribes for their votes. The average price was $300 for a vote, though in their final settlements, very few seemed to have realized in full the amounts promised. H. G. Worthington, under a promise of the Collectorship in Charleston – which appointment he afterwards obtained – was Patterson's indefatigable and unscrupulous "right-hand man," throughout the canvass.

The other candidates were R. B. Elliott, a colored representative, and R. K. Scott. In favor of Elliott was the fact that he was a representative colored man, and the majority of the Legislature were of that race. Scott had been paving the way for this personal promotion for years back, as Governor, etc. Patterson held no official position whatever, but was only known as an adroit and successful lobbyist. His only chance in the race then was money, and the testimony shows how lavishly he expended it. How much it cost him will probably never be known; but Senator Nash testifies, under oath, that Patterson told him after the election, that he had expended $40,000 in bribes, and that he had been forced to sell all his Blue Ridge Scrip, and mortgage his real estate in Columbia to raise the amount. (Page 918,) On the same point, John A. Barker, member from Edgefield, testified that Patterson told him personally that a certain amount of money – seventy-five thousand dollars, if necessary – was ready on hand to secure his election, and then offered him $1,000 for his own vote, and $2,000 additional, if he would secure the votes of two others of his delegation, the money to be paid at the bank as soon as the vote was cast. (Page 879.)

Of the seventy-five witnesses examined, sixty testified to direct tenders of bribes – in most cases accepted too – and yet, Mr. Collector Worthington stated, under oath, before the committee, that he had "no knowledge or information that money was used to secure the election of Patterson, save that he heard rumors of that kind on the streets." (Page 935.) Alarmed at one time, Patterson offered, through Gen. Dennis, to bribe Elliott himself off the field, with $15,000. This is established by the testimony of Elliott himself, who expressed much virtuous indignation at the base proposal.

After the Election,

earnest efforts were made to bring Patterson before the courts. He was immediately arrested, under a warrant for bribery, and sent to jail, whence he was promptly released on *Habeas Corpus,* by Judge Mackey. After a preliminary hearing before a Trial Justice, he was bound over to appear before the next Circuit Court. But Patterson laughed and snapped his finger at all this. Moses, as Governor, had already removed the jury commissioner, and had appointed Gen. Dennis in his stead. Judge Carpenter, Patterson's intimate friend, had just been elected to the bench, and Columbia belonged to his circuit. As to the juries in prospect, Gen. Dennis himself testified before the Committee: "When listing the juries for the year – grand and petit – I did not allow any name to go into the box in any way inimical to Patterson. In this way there could be no possibility of an enemy being drawn on either panel." (Page 936.)

And so his case has stood from that day to this. When the judiciary was reformed in 1876, as well as the Legislature, a serious effort was made to bring Patterson to trial, on this, as well as some other indictments. But a requisition on the proper authorities at Washington was judicially refused.

In view of the vast amount of crime and fraud unearthed by their very protracted and thorough investigation, the Committee recommend that judicial proceedings be at once begun against the most prominent on the foregoing list of thieves and defaulters. As to the spirit in which this should be done, they say, "and let this be undertaken in no temper of vengeance, not to gratify any morbid sentiment that would gloat over the sufferings of the criminal, overtaken by the sad consequences of his crime. But let it be done in the spirit of the patriot and the statesman – the spirit of the law, as expressed by the old Roman jurist and orator, '*ut pæna ad paucos, metus ad omnes perveniat;*' and as we learn it in the forcible words of the great expositor of the English Common Law, 'the end or final cause of human punishment is not by way of atonement or expiation of the crime committed – for that must be left to the just determination of the Supreme Being – but as a precaution against further offences of the same kind.'" (Page 886.)

The action of the Legislature, under this recommendation, caused the Attorney-General to begin proceedings – so far, with the following

Results.

More than thirty "True Bills" have been found by Grand Juries of Richland County – not very much varied in their character – and covering a long list of names. Sometimes five or six names would be embraced under the same indictment, and sometimes the same name would be found several times repeated. For instance, the name of Cardozo will be found on *nine* separate indictments.

With this explanation, only the following names can now be found on the Docket: H. H. Kimpton, D. H. Chamberlain, R. K. Scott, F. J. Moses, N. G. Parker, F. L. Cardozo, Robert Smalls, J. L. Neagle, F. S. Jacobs, (Solomon's Bank,) B. F. Whittemore, Solomon L. Hoge, Y. J. P. Owens, Thos. C. Dunn,

R. H. Gleaves, Samuel J. Lee, Josephus Woodruff, A. O. Jones and L. Cass Carpenter.

Of these, Parker, L. Cass Carpenter, Cardozo and Smalls, have been tried and convicted, on one indictment each; so far, the other criminals have not been very accessible.

Immunity has been granted to very many – mostly members of the Legislature – as in the seventy-five examined in Patterson's case.

In other cases, as Woodruff's, Jones', Nash's, and some others, promises of restitution were exacted and complied with, and thus the State was relieved of a large amount of indebtedness by the surrender of papers. How much, if any, money was refunded, has never come to light.

Personals.

Hiram H. Kimpton. – Two indictments in his case – one associating him with Patterson and Parker, for "conspiracy" to bribe members of the Legislature – and the other simply of "conspiracy," associating him with Chamberlain, Parker, Neagle and Leslie. (What single State could have withstood *such* a conspiracy as this?) A requisition on the Governor of Massachusetts was made for Kimpton, not long since, but her constituted authorities could not consent to the abduction of the embodiment of so much native financial ability from the borders of that State.

D. H. Chamberlain is also under indictment in the same court; but whether he will ever be tried is doubtful – and, if tried, whether he can be convicted, is still more doubtful. The slang expression of "running into a hole, and then drawing in the hole after him," is peculiarly appropriate to his course, all through his carpet-bag career. He has been the Alpha and Omega of Radicalism in South Carolina. Furnishing most of the brain in their first constitutional convention, serving as Attorney-General in their first administration, he was among the last of the office-holders to leave the State. A large shareholder in the "Printing Company," in the G. & C. R. R., in Solomon's Bank, and "attorney in fact" for several of the head devils in rascality, – yet he has managed always to keep himself behind the scenes, till his innate cunning would give him the cue. So well did he act his part, that even in 1876, when the "straightout" policy finally prevailed, there were many of our prominent citizens and newspapers who advocated Chamberlain, as the *Conservative* candidate for Governor. We can only say, that if Patterson reached the United States Senate on his peculiar carpet-bag merits, on the same ground, Daniel H. Chamberlain ought to be President for life.

R. K. Scott's eight years' career has already been very fully given in these pages. He has never been tried, though there are more than one of the indictments awaiting him. He has returned to his native Ohio, where old Judge Tucker once said the prevailing classes were the white man and the hog. With all his ill-gotten wealth, R. K. S. will never reach the F. F. O's.

B. F. Whittemore. – As senator from Darlington, his career in that county was even more diabolical than that of Joe Crews in Laurens. He retained his seat in the Senate, even after Chamberlain had abdicated as Governor. Finding the Investigating Committee hot on his trail, he applied for and received leave of absence to visit his "sick family" in Massachusetts. *Pairing with a member of this Investigating Committee in the Senate,* he took the train, and has not been seen or heard from since.

N. G. Parker. – Tried and convicted in the summer of 1875, under an indictment of "Larceny, and breach of trust, with fraudulent intent." Escaped from jail; was recaptured, and finally pardoned for that offense on promise to tell all he knew. There are five other indictments against him, and he has departed to parts unknown.

L. Cass Carpenter, editor and sympathizing lobbyist, was tried and convicted on an indictment of "Forgery." Pardoned, as to that case, by the Governor, on a petition carried around the Democratic Legislature by his wife, in person, in which it was asserted that his life would be endangered by his longer incarceration, as his health was very feeble. There are still four other indictments against him, and all for the same crime. Recently, at

Washington, and elsewhere, the papers represent him as devoting his spared life to abusing and vilifying those to whose clemency he is indebted for his life.

Y. J. P. Owens, senator from Laurens, indicted more than once for "conspiracy to cheat by false tokens," left his country for his country's good, and after wasting his ill-gotten substance in riotous living, died miserably in some Northern city, from excessive debauchery.

Francis L. Cardozo was tried and convicted by a jury of his own race, of "conspiracy." The President and Clerk of the Senate, and the Speaker and Clerk of the House, were associated with him in this indictment, but not in the trial. He was released on bail, pending his appeal for a new trial; and when this was refused, he returned and gave himself up. He was finally pardoned as to that case; but there are eight other indictments against him, on the same docket, embracing about all the fraudulent charges known to the judiciary. He is now happy in the Treasury Department in Washington, appointed under the Civil Service Reform Policy of President Hayes, for entire proficiency in all financial operations.

Robert Smalls, late member of Congress. His political influence was owing, mainly, to his being head bribe-broker for his Congressional District. He was tried and convicted on an indictment for bribery. His release was precisely similar to Cardozo's; and, with him, he is sharing the munificent fruits of President Hayes' Civil Service Reform.

S. A. Swails, senator from Williamsburg, and there having the same sway and infamous notoriety, as Whittemore, in Darlington, and Joe Crews, in Laurens, was not indicted in Richland, but promised immunity, if he would vacate his Presidency of the Senate, make restitution, and go and sin no more. (Gleaves, Lieutenant-Governor, and *ex-officio* President of the Senate, had already vacated his seat, and on the same terms). Instead of manifesting any penitence, Swails returned to his county, and became so desperately incendiary in his course, that the citizens very unanimously invited him to leave. After this, getting his carpet-bag filled with grievances and persecutions, he, too, went to Washington, and sat down with Cardozo and Smalls. Finding his quarters so comfortable, he sent word to his friend,

Sam Lee, of Sumter, another local politician of the same complexion and principles, to raise some row at home, and come on for his reward. This, Sam was not slow to do, and to-day, is sitting at the financial fountain of greenbacks. It is a strange sight, even in these days of political wonders, to behold Cardozo, Smalls, Swails and Lee flying from the penitentiary at home, to the hospitable shelter of the United States Treasury.

As an appropriate base for this column of notorious knaves, it is only necessary to write the name of

Franklin J. Moses.

It must be borne in mind, that the work of this Committee was confined to a particular class of frauds. Very little investigation was had into the "Bond" question, and none whatever into the infamous "Land Commission," with *C. P. Leslie* at its head. If the attempt should ever be made to publish *all* these frauds to the world, in the language of the Evangelist, it might be said, "I suppose that even the world itself could not contain the books that should be written."

Made in the USA
Columbia, SC
21 December 2018